The visual in learning and creativity: a review of the literature

A report for Creative Partnerships
Carey Jewitt
Institute of Education
University of London

Foreword

Creative Partnerships is the Government's flagship creative learning programme, designed to develop the skills of young people across England, raising their aspirations and achievements and opening up more opportunities for their futures.

The programme supports thousands of innovative, long-term partnerships between schools and creative professionals, from architects to scientists, multi-media developers to artists. They inspire schools to deliver the curriculum through innovative teaching techniques, and young people to challenge themselves in new ways, gain confidence and take an active role in their learning. Young people develop the skills they need to perform well not only in exams and extra-curricular activities, but also in the workplace and wider society. Working with Creative Partnerships, schools use creativity to solve problems and see real improvements in pupil behaviour and school performance.

Creative Partnerships aims to influence policy and practice in both the education and cultural sectors. It is managed by Arts Council England, with funding from the Department for Culture, Media and Sport (DCMS) and the Department for Children, Schools and Families (DCSF) in response to the National Advisory Committee on Creative and Cultural Education (NACCCE) report by Ken Robinson – *All Our Futures: Creativity, Culture and Education* (1999). The partnerships supported by Creative Partnerships are designed to develop creativity and encompass social, personal and economic domains. As a flagship project, Creative Partnerships can have maximum impact if teachers, parents, young people and creative practitioners learn from the experience and activities that are delivered through the programme. For this reason one of the most significant legacies of Creative Partnerships will be the product of its research and evaluation and how that is effectively communicated to stakeholders.

However, because Creative Partnerships works by creating partnerships drawn from the widest fields of endeavour, the different stakeholders recognise that there is a 'knowledge gap' between reflection, analysis and learning from Creative Partnerships. In addition, the wide focus of approach – which is fundamental to the nature of creativity - means that people are often working at the limit of their disciplines.

For these reasons we have commissioned a series of research monographs exploring the key issues in current literature and summarising the latest developments in each subject. Each monograph is written by an experienced and respected author in their field. The reports aim to be accessible, clearly referenced and to act as 'stepping-stone' resources to underpin the research conducted by and for Creative Partnerships.

This report offers an historical and theoretical overview of the 'turn to the visual' in late modern society. It examines changes in the communication landscape over the last 10-15 years and shows how young people in particular are now working, learning and living with a greater variety and richness of communicative tools. It explores how these changes have been approached, analysed and theorised and especially focuses on how such transformations make us re-think the processes of teaching and learning. This topic is highly relevant to the ambitions, scope and reach of Creative Partnerships and Carey Jewitt helps us further in this aim by teasing out some of the relationships between curriculum design and delivery and creative learning. Her key messages are that education not only needs to understand better the diversity and reach of young people's multimodal worlds but that any education system which aspires to be creative needs to lead curriculum and pedagogy on this basis.

We hope that the report will be a useful and practical handbook for those interested in better understanding how the 'turn to the visual' underpins changing practice in teaching and learning. It offers a serious and sophisticated review of key concepts and a comprehensive and original review of how we can make use of communication changes at practical and theoretical levels. If Creative Partnerships wants to leave a lasting impact on schools and the curriculum through its distinct and different ways of working and pushing the boundaries of how we understand learning, it needs to engage with the challenges Carey Jewitt lays out so clearly for us.

Dr David Parker, Creative Partnerships
Dr Julian Sefton-Green, Creative Partnerships

Introduction

A visual world?

Everyday life in the 21st century is saturated with image, visual technologies and visual practices. A wide range of production and distribution technologies circulate a variety of visual materials - photographs, video and diverse media through blogs, online photo albums, YouTube, MySpace and so on. Still images stare out across the everyday communicational landscape and moving images try to grab attention through a multiplicity of devices, enabling people to easily share their digital stories across global networks. The visual turn can be understood as a response to this newly configured global and networked landscape marked by the social, cultural and economic trajectories of late (post) modernity: fluidity, speed, saturation, frenzied pixilation, and immediacy (Bauman, 1998; Castells, 2001).

The terrain of communication, creativity and education is changing in profound ways. Traditional uses of literacy and associated means for representing and communicating are mutating at every level and in every domain (Kress, 2003). These changes are, however, occurring to different degrees and at uneven rates (Luke and Carrington, 2002). As a consequence it is no longer possible to think about learning and literacy solely as 'linguistic' accomplishments: the time for that habitual conjunction of 'language and learning' is over. This has significant implications for communication, creativity, education and the design of social futures for the 21st century (New London Group, 1996; Gee, Hull and Lankshear, 1996; Gee, 2004; Luke and Carrington, 2002; Kress, 2003).

In order to better understand the opportunities and challenges for creativity and learning in the contemporary visual (or multimodal[1]) context, it is therefore essential to explore how image and other symbolic forms of representation feature in schools.

Scope and structure of this review

This review addresses the question 'How does the turn to the visual affect contemporary notions of creativity and education?' In order to address this question the review of the literature is organised into four sections.

Section 1: A turn to the visual: This section provides a brief history of the visual turn. The question of why the visual turn has come about at this point in time is explored. The need to understand visual communication as a part of a broader move toward non-linguistic forms of communication is discussed.

---

[1] Multimodality (Kress and van Leeuwen, 2001), asserts the need to understand visual and linguistic communication in the broader communicational landscape they occur within, including gesture, gaze, posture and so on. See section 1.3 for an introduction to this approach and its key ideas.

Section 2: The scope of the visual in education is briefly outlined in section two, specifically, the notion of multiple intelligences (2.1); followed by a commentary on how a visual lens can draw new attention to the visual design of learning spaces (2.2); the visual texts that circulate in spaces of learning (2.3); visual teaching (2.4); and visual practices that might lead to learning (2.5). This sketch sets the scene for part three of the review.

Section 3: Reconfiguring the visual landscape of education: This section centres on the discussion of six thematic areas identified within the literature which are key to the changing place of the visual within creativity and education in contemporary society: the access that learners have to a broader range of representational forms and multimodal configurations (3.1); the changing sites of display for learners (3.2); the ways in which these combine to re-shape knowledge (3.3); new conditions for authorship (3.4); changing practices in production and dissemination (3.5); and the new skills required by young people in a changed and changing media landscape (3.6).

Section 4: Visual Futures: This part moves on to ask what this reconfigured communicational landscape means for creativity and learning, with specific attention to: new opportunities for learner identity formation and management (4.1); literacy (4.2); and teaching (4.3).

Finally, the review concludes with a summary of the key points, challenges and questions presented for creativity and education by a turn to the visual.

This review provides an indicative map of the literature and its key themes as they relate to the turn to the visual for creativity and education. The literature review synthesises a wide variety of sources across a range of disciplines including visual culture and communication, cultural and media studies with a focus on cultural forms and participation, art history, education, social psychology, sociology with a focus on media and technology and identity, and semiotics. Educational research studies are drawn on throughout the review as illustrative exemplars and models.

The next section provides the starting point for this review by investigating the background to the visual turn and situating it within the realm of education.

1 A turn to the visual

The phrase 'visual turn' is used in different and often contradictory ways – frequently with considerable hyperbole. This section gives a brief background to the 'visual turn' to provide an anchor point for the review and to place creativity and education in a broader social and cultural context. This is followed by a sketch of the visual scope of education to set the scene for the thematic discussion presented in sections two and three.

1.1 Background

The concept of the visual turn, also referred to as the pictorial turn (Mitchell, 1995:11), points to the fundamental role of the visual in society and culture, and the need to attend to visual manifestations of the social and cultural in order to understand society in general (Mirzoeff, 1999; Mitchell, 1995). Understanding how the visual both produces *and* represents culture is the reason attending to the visual forms of representation and communication is important for creativity and education. The key argument is that images act as 'go-betweens in social transactions' that 'structure our encounters' (Mitchell, 2002:175), as cultures of everyday life are entwined with practices of representation. Considering images from this perspective, the continuous circulation and repetition of images in the school and other educational spaces can be seen as actively working to define social and cultural norms (while simultaneously presenting these as fixed and natural). Understanding the visual and multimodal mediascapes[2] (Appadurai, 1990) that children and young people are immersed in and move across, as well as the visual resources that these mediascapes make available, is therefore a central aspect of supporting creativity and learning. For instance, the visual materials and objects that (are allowed to) enter learning environments embody and constitute the system of thoughts and beliefs that determine institutional expectations, actions and behaviours in ways that are important for creativity and education more broadly.

One consequence of the visual turn is that it draws attention not only to visual objects and materials but also to practices of looking. It serves to foreground how discipline and control can be achieved through relations of looking, as well as how power operates to control what or who is seen/ made visible and what or who is not (ideas initiated in the work of the sociologist Foucault, 1977[3]). The 'gaze' and what it means to look are commonly associated with the regulatory environment of the school (and elsewhere). A vision that

---

2 Appadurai (1990) combined the term 'scape' with 'media' to refer to the cultural flow of information across a communicational landscape that is irregular, fluid and realised through complex networks across local and global boundaries. Mediascape therefore refers to both the capabilities of production and dissemination of new media as well as the images of the world created by these media. It is used here to refer to the media and image landscapes (via which culture is realised) that young people occupy. This encompasses a broad range of media including television and film, music, comics, books, websites, games and so on.

can be understood on the one hand as an outcome of mechanisms of surveillance – the institutional gaze of the school - or on the other, its 'ethical alternative' of 'watching out for' or 'looking after someone' (Jay, 2002:89). A key point for education is that vision and gaze are a part of the orchestration of the social relations in learning environments, both formal and informal. It is in this way that the visual is central to the constitution of 'the student' or 'the learner' (or in a gallery or museum, the visitor). Prosser (2007) and Grosvenor (2007) examine how the visual culture of the school is produced in ways that are significant for the positioning of learners and teachers. They claim that through the interaction between the visual-spatial design of school – such as through visual materials, the school uniform, displays in corridors and classrooms, or the arrangement of furniture - particular configurations of 'the learner' are created or 'come into being'. The visual turn thus draws attention to both how an institutional gaze (such as that of the school) is materially shaped and, perhaps more importantly, how these might be re-designed to support alternative identities and learner positions.

1.2 Why now?

The visual turn can be seen as a representational manifestation of social changes in contemporary global society: changing relationships to truth and authority; new requirements and access to information and knowledge; the increasingly flexible or open nature of identity formation; the connections across local/national and global/international boundaries; as well as the development of new technologies and the visual representational and communicational possibilities that these make available. These new social conditions change how the visual features in people's lives.

Up until the 20th century an interest in visual representation was primarily associated with art and art history. The focus was on the artist's intention or the viewers' perception. In the latter half of the 20th century, however, there was a broadening of interest in visual representation to include the everyday images that surrounded people. This included seminal studies of image in film (Metz, 1990), the use of photography (Sontag, 1979), advertising (Goffman, 1979), scientific imagery (Latour and Woolgar, 1986), learning (Kress, 1996), and the representation of social identities (Hall, 1997). People's everyday experience of the world - socially, physically and psychologically - was shown as strongly mediated by the visual.

---

[3] Foucault in 'Discipline and Punishment: The birth of the Prison' (1977) compares modern society to the 'panopticon' design, used in prisons, in which a single unseen observer can watch over the many – who do not know/can not tell if they are being watched at a particular moment. It is through visibility, Foucault argues, that modern society exercises its systems of power to discipline and regulate subjects. Foucualt thus presents a vision of society in which people in a position of power use their gaze to survey and apply norms of acceptable behavior to others. He argues that these ideas are as applicable to teachers in educational sites as they are to prison guards.

Visual representation was clearly revealed to be crucial to *how* people experience the world, and therefore to how the world itself is constructed.

The visual turn has its roots in the work of the British cultural studies movement[4] (e.g. Hall, 1997; Berger, 1972; Mulvey, 1989)[5]. The idea of the visual turn developed momentum in the 1980s and early 1990s both as a symptom of, and a response to, the social and technological conditions of contemporary society - specifically postmodernism and globalisation. Further development of the visual turn was pursued by others (e.g. Mirzoeff, 1999; Jenks, 1995; Sturken and Cartwright, 2001; and Elkins, 2003) including, perhaps most notably, W.T.J Mitchell (1995). By the 1990s the visual turn was established as a key concept in cultural studies and new media and communication studies, while visual studies itself was emerging as a new academic discipline[6]. This work has filtered into research and practice within creativity and education.

Much has been written about the particular dominance of the visual in contemporary society. Indeed it has been argued that the modern world has become a visual phenomenon that conflates looking, seeing and knowing (Jenks, 1995) - a kind of 'vision machine' created through new visualising technologies in which people are all caught (Virilio, 1994). Mitchell (2002, 2005a) asks, however, if this characterisation is true. He asks this question to refute two important criticisms of the visual turn. First, that the visual turn does not engage with the past, leading to the a-historical claim that the contemporary communicational landscape is more visual era than previous eras. Second, that the term is euro-centric in describing contemporary (digital) western societies as *more* visual than others. In his book *What do Pictures Want?* (2005b), Mitchell takes an historical view and argues that the visual turn is not new, recalling the illuminated manuscripts of medieval times, the complex iconographic paintings of the past and so on. In a similar vein, Burns and Dixon (2005) argue that subject English as it is taught in schools has 'a long and intimate relationship with the visual' including specially-illustrated editions of novels and poetry such as Dickens and Milton, picture books, graphic novels, comic strips and manga[7], as well as film, television and computer games (Burn and Dixon, 2005:1). Mitchell argues that the visual or pictorial turn can be more usefully understood as a repeated narrative that marks 'specific moments when a new medium, a technical invention, or a cultural practice erupts in symptoms of panic or euphoria (usually both) about the

---

[4] This emerged from the Birmingham School of Contemporary Cultural Studies in the 1970s and its focus on media and popular visual cultural texts such as television, film and fashion.

[5] According to Elkins (2003) the term – visual turn – was first coined by the art historian Michael Baxandall in 1973 in his book Painting and Experience in Fifteenth Century Italy, Oxford: Oxford University Press.

[6] As witnessed by the number of new anthologies, readers and journals on the visual.

[7] Japanese comic books read by children and adults in Japan, serialising stories that deal with a wide range of adult themes and narrative genres.

visual' (Mitchell, 2002:173). His argument resonates with polarised educational debates in which the visual staggers between accusations of aiding an abhorrent 'dumbing down' of knowledge or rescuing education from anachronism[8].

Mitchell's understanding of the visual turn as a commentary on new ways of making images and the marking of a historical turning point is significant and productive for creativity and education for three reasons. First, this approach to the visual turn refuses to confine visuality to the modern era and in doing so it connects the contemporary with the past. This enables patterns and narratives of the visual to be seen over time and for connections to be made with respect to practices across different technologies. Second, it acknowledges that to live in *any* culture is to live in a visual culture and therefore it extends discussion beyond western societies. This more inclusive definition is key for understanding creativity and education in diverse contexts as it refuses the denial of non-western culture and opens up a space for acknowledging difference. Third, this perspective on the visual turn moves away from the (easy) construction of binary models of history that centre on a turning point and 'declare a single great divide between the age of literacy (for instance) and the age of visuality' (Mitchell, 2003:173). When combined, these three points demand that attention be paid to the specificity of how visual and other symbolic forms are configured and elaborated in different historical, social and cultural contexts. This marks an important departure away from questions about the extent to which image dominates word or vice versa, instead sharpening our focus on *how* the visual is configured and put to work for the purposes of education and society– and how the visual may be put to work in different ways to produce different effects.

While the visual is a central aspect of representation and communication it is not only the visual that is implicated in the need to look beyond language. Mitchell (2005b) argues for the mixed hybrid character of media and the impossibility of engaging in a purely visual medium, in that the visual always exists/operates alongside other modes and that there is no pure visual perception.

---

[8] For example, debates rage about the impact of computer games on young people's creativity and learning: on the one hand they have been accused of destroying childhood practices of reading, reducing attention spans and over-stimulating children. On the other hand, there have been debates on how the motivational factors of games can be harnessed to enhance learning in the school.

1.3 Beyond the visual?

The assumption that meanings are made, distributed, interpreted and remade, through many representational and communicational resources, of which language is but one, is key to multimodality (Kress and van Leeuwen, 2001). The concept of multimodality attends to the visual in configurations across gesture, gaze, body posture, sound, writing, music, speech and so on (for a full discussion of multimodal theory see Kress and van Leeuwen, 2001; Norris, 2004; Jewitt, 2006). As a result of decades of classroom language research, much is known about the resources of language yet considerably less is understood about the potentials of other forms of representation. However, detailed studies have helped begin to describe the resources and organising principles of image (Kress and van Leeuwen, 2006), sound (Van Leeuwen, 1999), writing (Kenner, 2004; Kenner and Kress, 2003), and how these all work together in multimodal ensembles (see Kress *et al*, 2001, 2005; Flewitt, 2006).

This work argues that people select from, adapt and orchestrate the wide range of resources that are available to them to make meaning in specific contexts. Flewitt's (2006) multimodal study of preschool classroom interaction, for instance, demonstrates the strong link between the forms of communication people use and the context they are in - in this case the nursery, the home, and the modes young children use to communicate. Her research draws on video case studies of young children communicating at home and in a preschool playgroup. Through detailed multimodal analysis of the interaction of a child who is silent in nursery and talkative at home, Flewitt shows how talk with siblings and in the home contrast with talk in the nursery setting. She shows how the structures of the classroom and home scaffold talk in different ways, and argues for the need to attend to children's multimodal communication while warning against 'pathologising the absence of talk' (Flewitt, 2006:47). This comprehensive analysis looks beyond language and the visual to account for gesture, space, body values the wide range of resources that children and young people bring to learning and examines how these resources are shaped by the specificity of the context.

Multimodality asserts that all modes are partial. Each contributes to the production of knowledge in distinct ways and therefore no one mode stands alone in the process of making meaning, rather each plays a discrete role in the whole: hence the need to attend to all.

In summary, the 21st century can be viewed as an historical moment when technology aids the production and circulation of images at an 'unimagined level' (Jay, 2002:88). This requires an understanding of how images and other non-linguistic forms are used within education as part of broader social and cultural work.

2 The scope of the visual in education

In many areas of education there has been a lack of attention to visual and other non-linguistic resources. Children's visual representations are rarely developed and built on as a means for future communication (Kress, 1997). In general, pictures, the design elements of writing, and other visual forms are held in low esteem and the move from pictures to words is seen as 'one of intellectual progression' in which 'drawing becomes regarded as a dispensable embellishment' (Millard and Marsh, 2001:55). Where image is acknowledged in educational settings it is often celebrated for its potential to interest and motivate learners and the link between visual forms of knowledge and learning is seldom made. To some extent then, the visual and multimodal survive at the margins of the curriculum (Millard and Marsh, 2001). This is a paradox. As this section will demonstrate, educational spaces are highly visual and multimodal environments.

2.1 Visual intelligence

The theory of Multiple Intelligences, introduced by Gardner in 1983, has been influential within education although it has been strongly criticised by some academics and practitioners as serving to pigeonhole learners and being difficult to implement in the context of assessment, examination and league tables. Gardner argued against theories of a general intelligence, which emphasises mathematical logic and knowledge retention and is commonly measured by the IQ test. Instead, he proposed seven distinct intelligences[9] of which visual-spatial intelligence is one. He suggested that each person has a unique 'cognitive profile' which leads them to have different kinds of intelligences and which demand a personalised approach to learning.

The goal to broaden the notion of intelligence beyond linguistic and mathematical logics speaks to current educational agendas in several ways: issues of inclusion and social justice, the need to respect diversity, to engage with the abilities of all students, to personalise learning, and the need to provide a broad and rich curriculum that motivates and connects with students' interests. The notion of multiple intelligence not only maps easily onto these agendas but also affirms teachers' common sense knowledge and experience that people learn in different ways and that a variety of activities and approaches to a topic can often be more effective than a universal one.

---

[9] The other six categories of intelligence he labelled are linguistic, musical, logical-mathematical, bodily-kinaesthetic, interpersonal and intra personal although he makes clear that these categories are not exhaustive and more recently added naturalistic intelligence (Gardner, 1999).

The notion of 'learning styles' - that is where learners are understood to fall into modality types - has developed in response to Gardner's work. In turn, this has led to the notion of 'visual learners': people who learn through seeing and think in pictures and are therefore thought to be best taught using visual displays, diagrams and so on[10]. There are many books aimed at educators which show how to render curricular topics into modally specific representations and activities to appeal to distinct modality types, and these ideas have seeped into educational policy.

Although both visual-spatial intelligence and the visual learner are dominant ideas in current education, leading figures within psychology, cognitive neuroscience and educational theory have strongly and persistently critiqued these ideas as unhelpful, and as theoretically and empirically unfounded. Five key criticisms are made concerning the assumptions and methods that underpin multiple intelligences: 1) that which Gardner describes is not intelligences but abilities or talents; 2) these theories are based on rhetoric, hunch and opinion, with no empirical studies to offer evidence of the validity of multiple intelligences; 3) the method (a questionnaire) deployed to establish multiple intelligences is ad-hoc and does not account for developmental stages; 4) it does not explain variation in intelligence; and 5) even if there are different intelligences, a general intelligence would entail being good at each of them (Klein, 2003). Multiple intelligence has also been criticised by educationalists on the grounds that it can lead to intellectual relativism, be used to 'explain' or excuse poor progress in learning and naturalise failure, and that it can lead to reduced incentives for those students labelled as particular kinds of learners to study for some subjects. In addition, the classification of learners has been described as a 'fatal simplification' that is neither based on sound theory or empirical evidence (Klein, 2003). Franklin (2006) argues that while multiple intelligences is a dominant theme in education, instead of drawing attention to how children learn it has led to labelling learners. Franklin's call for increased debate and interrogation of the concept is an urgent one in a context where being labelled a 'visual' or 'kinaesthetic' learner appears increasingly to be a code for 'low ability'.

---

[10] As well as visual learners, according to Gardner there are also auditory learners and kinaesthetic learners.

2.2 Visual design of learning spaces and visual displays

The architecture of a school, museum, gallery or other educational space does not determine what happens within it. Rather, it shapes interaction through the way it operates 'as a set of pathways and constraints, facilitating and frustrating parts of the educational mission' (Prosser, 2007:15). The visual culture of learning spaces is in part built into the material structure of a building and in part made through the interactions that occur within it (Seaborne, 1977; Grosvenor *et al*, 1999). In other words, the everyday behaviours of people both shape *and* are shaped by the cultures that are realised visually in the physicality of a building as well as in the patterned social interactions that form its social culture. For instance, most schools in the UK include teacher spaces, student spaces, spaces designated for play or leisure, while others are designated as learning spaces, including some with specialised purposes (e.g. science labs or computer suites). These designated functions are realised physically (through the arrangement of the space, the furniture used, the objects that are made available), as well as socially (through norms and rules concerning who is permitted to enter etc).

The visual turn draws attention to the design and use of learning spaces. In the *View of the Child* project (Burke, 2007), researchers worked with children to investigate their awareness, understanding, experiences and desires for the school as a designed space, later expanding their work to include museums and galleries. This research confirms the importance of the design of places to learn as setting the framework for participation and a sense of learning.

Visual displays are a feature of most UK educational environments. These are often discussed in relation to how they create an attractive environment for learning. From a more critical perspective, visual displays can be charged with naturalising the learning environment and with making opaque the exercising of power (Foucault, 1977). For example, the visual references that are included or excluded in a classroom display draw the boundaries around a subject and a learning space– such as the quiet exclusion of images from popular culture in many classroom displays. The design of learning environments, the arrangements of space and the use of displays do not remain an 'inert' or 'pre-created' background to the work of a lesson or session. Rather, they are activated and re-activated by the students and the teacher. In this respect, the teacher's role (teacher is used here in the broadest sense) is central: the teacher mediates what is displayed and what is enacted in the classroom and it is the teacher who connects the display to the topic being taught (Daniels, 2001:169). These displays, as they are brought into the lesson by the teacher, relay the curriculum and disciplinary rules of the school or other sites of learning (see Figure 1). They provide a framework of what is to be learnt and what is valued, which then shapes how learners are expected to behave. Visual displays and the arrangement of the classroom can therefore be understood as a teaching tool, a medium to communicate desired qualities and expectations, in a manner that is to be lived by the students (Kress and van Leeuwen, 2001).

Figure 1.
The visualising of disciplinary warnings in a primary school classroom. The pegs with names on represent the children in the classroom. © Carey Jewitt

Different images are allowed into some learning contexts and others not, and are mobilised for the purposes of teaching and learning in distinct ways. Research on the multimodal production of secondary school English (Kress *et al*, 2005; Jewitt and Jones, 2005) demonstrated how teachers' multimodal design of the classroom environment operated to convey what was to be done and learnt within it, and the place of students' life worlds of 'English' (i.e. the kinds of texts they engage with, the functions of English in the texts they engage with, the interactions they participate in, and the social environments they inhabit). Across nine teacher case studies, the design of each classroom connected with the life worlds of students and teachers differently. One case study teacher covered the walls with posters of film and music stars brought in by the students, for instance; another displayed carefully framed elements drawn from curriculum and examination documents; while another displayed posters of poetry and art exhibitions. These visual displays realised different versions of English (and Englishness) that operated to place students in different relationships to the curriculum content. In turn these displays attempted to connect or disconnect English as a subject to the experiences of those students in ways that are significant for the construction of literacy. The visual displays and spatial arrangement of these English classrooms can be understood as multimodal signs mediating a diversity of historical and cultural scripts. They are sets of 'potentials' that hint at certain possibilities and offer particular constraints, while influencing what happens in the classroom. However, they do not determine what happens in the classroom: the ways in which the teachers and students take up, resist, interpret, and remake the meanings of these potentials through their interaction is crucial.

The visual design of physical learning environments also applies to digital 'virtual' learning environments. Focusing on the visual construction of learning environments raises three questions for creativity and education. First, what do the texts, objects and furniture in a learning environment represent in relation to a curriculum subject? What is included? What resources are students offered for their learning and how are they positioned, 'physically' and conceptually, in relation to this knowledge? Secondly, how are visual and other non-symbolic forms used to represent the subject? What is the visual used to explore? Which modes are foregrounded and by what means? Thirdly, what is given importance or made central through the resources of visual display and spatial-temporal arrangements of a learning environment?

2.3 Visual materials in learning spaces

A wide range of visual materials (e.g. textbooks, work sheets, objects and models, drawings, websites) are consumed, produced, mobilised and circulated within all environments for learning – including the secondary school.

Children and young people regularly create physical and virtual visual objects and artefacts that are a part of learning and teaching both across the school curriculum and beyond. These include drawings, three-dimensional models, PowerPoint presentations, photographs, digital videos, websites and so on (see Figures 2 a-c). These visual materials feature across the curriculum, notably in the curriculum subjects of Science, Art and Design, Geography and Maths, but also in curricula spaces deemed linguistic, like English and History. Learning, especially in nursery and primary schools, is physical and tactile, involving the use of a variety of everyday and specialist objects, models and equipment. These may include computer-programmed objects that behave and respond in particular ways, and link to physical movement with visual representations (Price and Rogers, 2003). Meanwhile, virtual learning environments and simulation applications make available new conditions for action (e.g. suspended gravity) (Jewitt, 2006).

Figure 2a

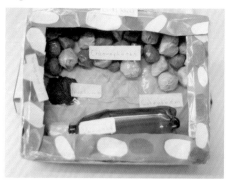

Figure 2b

Figure 2c

Figures 2a, 2b, and 2c.
A selection of three-dimensional models of a plant cell made by Year 7 secondary school students for Science homework using a variety of materials.
© Carey Jewitt

Up until the last decade or so, however, these resources have received little attention, within research and pedagogic communities, with images relegated to mere illustration. That said, there appears to be an increased interest in the role of the visual in children's learning, with growing recognition of its potential for engaging learners with the visual aspects of writing and reading, as well as students' production of multimodal models and digital multimedia materials (Kress, 2003; Kenner, 2004; Bearne, 2003; Bearne and Wolstencroft, 2007; Burn and Parker, 2003; Pahl, 2006; Stein, 2007). Indeed a substantial body of work now exists on the role of image in children's books, the relationship between pictures and writing (Walsh, 2000), and on how students navigate these materials through the creation of reading pathways that rely on pictures, colour and other graphical elements and layout (Moss, 2003) (see sections 4.3 through to 4.5 for fuller discussion).

Images and visual objects, visual experiences and practices are common in the classroom and have a central role in how knowledge is presented, and support dialogue and interaction between learners. In school Science, teachers use image and visual technologies to represent scientific ideas in ways that make objects, phenomena and relationships visible (Lemke, 1998; Kress et al, 2001; Lynch, 2006). Observation and drawing are, and have been for many years, central to the teaching and learning of science (Reiss et al, 2007; Scott and Jewitt, 2003; Kress et al, 2001). Geography teachers can draw on maps and a broad range of visual and spatial representations, including those made by students. More recently, teachers can utilise digital representations via programmes such as GoogleEarth and other Geographical Information Systems (GIS), as well as mobile technologies (NRC, 2006; Kerski, 2003). Even in the English classroom, where common sense would have it that language is what really matters, teaching and learning are realised visually (Kress et al 2005; Jewitt 2006). In the English classroom, speech and writing are enmeshed with images, photographs, video excerpts downloaded from the Internet, illustrations in anthologies and novels, teacher drawings on whiteboards, as well as the images, sound, music and animation used in DVDs and CD-ROMS. Digital video - easily accessed via internet connected interactive whiteboards (IWBs) - is increasingly used in the English classroom and has been found to support students writing and awareness of narrative structures in a medium that young people use in their everyday experiences (Reid, 2003). Digital technologies, such as interactive whiteboards have the potential to act as a multimodal digital hub in the classroom (Moss et al, 2007). Further, an internet-connected IWB can make available new temporal and spatial connections across sites of learning, linking the classroom with museums and other specialised centres (Ball, 2003; Miller, 2003). It is now common to see an English lesson starting with a short video on YouTube, or a Science lesson examining a collection of artefacts in a museum or information from the NASA website. The use of IWBs in lessons can also open up new possiblities for student interaction with images, such as manipulating images, remixing them, incorporating them in new texts (Glover *et al*, 2005; Kennewell and Beauchamp, 2007).

Physical and digital visual technologies proliferate in the school: from microscope to visualiser. These technologies enable the everyday to be viewed in new ways and for some things to be made newly visible. Mavers' (2008) research on the use of a visualiser (attached to either a projector or interactive whiteboard) in primary school settings, shows how this visual technology can be used to display a variety of objects (e.g. students' exercise books, a page from a text book, a shell or a leaf) at a large scale to the whole class. Digital images from visualisers and scanners can be annotated, manipulated and stored. Mavers (2008) research raises new questions in relation to how we understand teaching and learning, for instance how students understand and work with issues of scale.

The visual turn prompts us to examine how changes in media affect learning processes, and how the visual can be harnessed to the purposes of creativity and education.

2.4 Visual and multimodal teaching

Significant pedagogic work is realised visually and through a range of non-linguistic modes, rather than being merely supportive or illustrative of what is said.

A number of projects have purposively introduced image into educational contexts in order to develop forms of teaching and learning beyond language. Stein (2003), for example, explored the relations between creativity, multimodal pedagogy, representation and learning in research with children living in informal settlements in South Africa. Students used 2D drawings, writing, 3D figures, spoken dialogues and performance to create narratives of identity and culture. The focus was on the representation of doll and child figures and their symbolic meanings (see Figure 3). These figures became the basis of story-telling narratives. Stein argued that the use of such visual objects in a multimodal pedagogy enables students' identity, cultural practices and community to enter the school context in ways that are significant for literacy and teaching.

Figure 3.
Contemporary doll/child figure produced by children in Johannesburg, South Africa as part of the 'Olifantsvlei Fresh Stories Project' facilitated and reported by Pippa Stein (2003).
© Pippa Stein

In an action research study of young people's literacy practices in a humanities class in New York, Walsh (2007) drew upon students' out-of-school experiences, by incorporating student proficiency as designers and producers of online texts, including the integration and orchestration of images. Students developed websites on the topic of migration (see Figure 4). The potential for open reading paths, and the use of images and layout, offered students possibilities to be creative in their exploration and expression of the topic. This work engaged students in the creation of new texts and forms of meaning, leading Walsh to design a curriculum that changed what counts as literacy work in his classroom (2007).

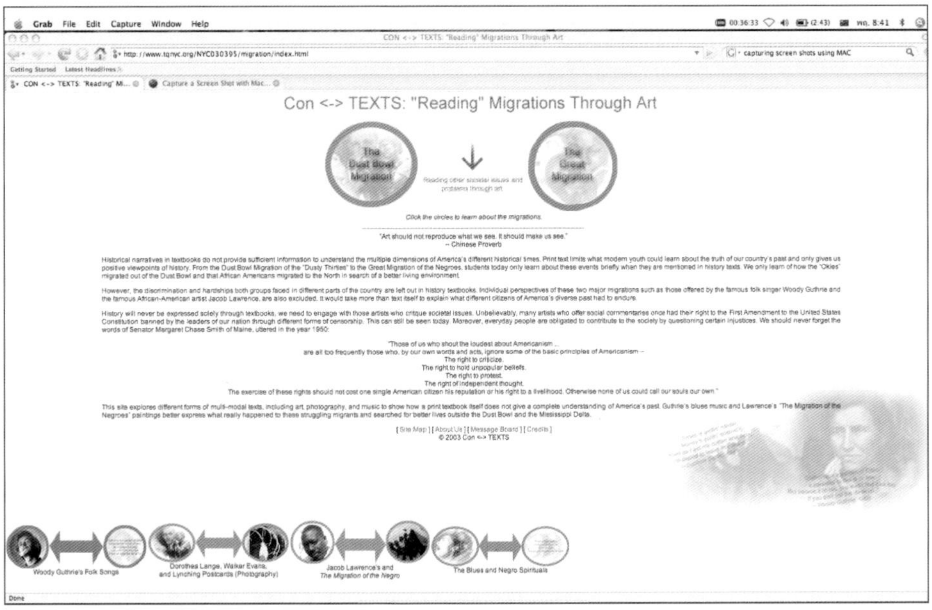

Figure 4.
This image shows a screen from a website designed by a group of five middle year students in school in New York City, USA, for a ThinkQuest competition entitled ConTexts: Reading two migrations through the arts as discussed by Christopher Walsh (2007).
© Chris Walsh

Research, such as the 'Multimodal Production of School English' project (Kress *et al*, 2005), has also illustrated the complex ways in which image, gesture, gaze, interaction with objects, body posture, writing and speech interact in the 'everyday' classroom production subject knowledge. Kress *et al*'s project highlights how students and teachers co-produce notions of ability, resistance and identity within the classroom through their non-verbal interaction. The classroom displays, artefacts, and the embodied practices of the teacher and students were orchestrated to realise versions of English as a specific school subject. This research shows that the process of interpretation and learning operates beyond merely language, and requires the ability to make sense of a range of modes and the relationships between them. For example, over a series of 12 lessons studying Macbeth, the students drew images, downloaded images and visual information, arranged images into the narrative sequence of the play, performed the play, and watched a film version of the play.

2.5 Visual and multimodal learning

The visual is a key feature in learning and the shaping of knowledge (for a fuller discussion of shapes of knowledge see section 4.3). Children's drawings, models and the other visual materials can be analysed to reveal the many ways in which they interpret and experience concepts. Reiss *et al* (2007) analysed drawings by 78 students (ranging from 5-14 years old) of the natural environment in a school Science lesson to examine their understanding of the natural world. Researchers analysed the elements represented, drawing styles, visual details, the degree of interconnectedness between elements, the use of scale, and the relationships established visually between animals, environment and plants (see Figure 5). Although many of these drawings would generally be understood as misconceptions, Reiss *et al* argue that taking children's drawings seriously can prove useful in revealing the diverse influences on children's production of knowledge and offers a way of engaging with students' experiences and views of the world. Their analysis revealed the presence of religious notions of nature, the Garden of Eden, and the 'Disneyfication of the environment', for example, in the form of smiling animals. Other studies have shown how the move from two dimensional image to concept-map or model, offer new resources to extend analogies and metaphors through colour, shape, movement, imported objects and texture (Kress *et al*, 2001).

Labels in the drawing: CLOUD, PIGEON, OAK TREE, SQUIRREL, ANT, DAISY, MUSHROOM, GRASS, POND

Figure 5.

A drawing produced by a 14 year old, showing nine objects which they were asked to draw in a Science lesson. The drawing is from a research project on the natural environment conducted by Michael Reiss, Carolyn Boulter and Sue Dale Tunnicliffe (2007).

Several studies have examined students' digital production to examine how the visual resources these make available contribute to the reshaping of learning (e.g. Pelletier, 2005; Leander, 2001, 2007; Burn and Parker, 2003; Sefton- Green, 2006), some of which are discussed in detail in sections 4.3 and 4.5 of this review. The process of learning is intricately related to the agency of the sign-maker, the technology used, and the visual and multimodal resources available. For example, in Jewitt's research (2003), two students designing a computer game, using the application Toontalk, about 'a little figure that will be caught by an alien', chose the most apt visual signifiers from the resources of image and movement available to them in order to express the relative vulnerability and strength of the characters in their game.

This section has provided a rough sketch of the visual in education. It has examined what it is that the visual turn can bring into focus and sets the scene for a fuller discussion of key themes in the visual landscape of creativity and education that is presented in section 4.

3 Reconfiguring the visual landscape of education

The turn to the visual calls for a recognition and interrogation of the role of the visual in creativity and education. It suggests the need to re-assess the place of the visual, and to re-evaluate its role and function. This is an imperative in a communicational landscape that is in a state of flux and change.

This section maps out six themes identified in the literature that are central to understanding the significance of the visual and multimodal landscape for creativity and education. These themes are 1) the access learners have to a broader range of representational resources and new multimodal ensembles; 2) the changing sites of display that young people are engaged with; 3) the ways in which the changing landscape affects new shapes of knowledge; 4) the new conditions and functions for authorship; 5) an increased emphasis on, as well as new forms of, visual production; and 6) new skills and practices for negotiating and navigating information and meanings in this multimodal landscape.

3.1 A range of resources and multimodal configurations

3.1.1 Access to a broad range of resources

The visual scope of education outlined in the previous section demonstrates that whatever the technology, learners and educators have access to a wide variety of visual resources. In the contemporary UK context, the majority of children and young people have some access to such facilities and are able to generate images, music, video clips, animations, and other non-linguistic materials through a range of physical and digital technologies (Kress, 2003; Jewitt, 2006; Marsh, 2006). These technologies bring image, colour, movement, sound, music and other modes into the classroom as resources for making meaning. Digital visual and multimodal representations, such as those made available through the use of mobile technologies and GIS systems, provide a range of new features that may support pupils' concept-development, learning and creativity (NRC, 2006; Kerski, 2003; Wiegand, 2001). The use of GoogleEarth in the Geography classroom, for example, enables students to zoom in and out, and thus view data at different scales and from different perspectives; students can produce multiple layers of data on specific locations; time-lines can be created to show change over time; and students can create hyperlinks to other materials, access textual or pictorial annotations, and generate their own maps. A focus on the visual asserts the need to understand how these representational and interactive features might be exploited to support student understanding and expression through their own production (see section 4.4). This introduces new visual resources -

transience and permanence, layers and overlays – which affect how students interpret and produce meaning.

Flexible, interactive and fluid hypertexts are a relatively new resource in the repertoire of making meaning. Hyperlinks increasingly align reading with the production and consumption of images alongside writing. The conceptual shift demanded by hypertext is, Luke (2003:400) suggests, from one of "collection to connection", a move that underlies the production of complex hybrid systems, new repertoires and demands for literacy. In this symbol-rich environment, reading is transformed. For instance, a digital novel can be realised as a multimodal configuration of music and songs, voices, sketches, maps and photographs, video clips, and written prose. Such multimodal texts re-make the conditions for students to read texts in different ways, for instance as a musical, a short film, a comic book or any other genre (Jewitt, 2002). In short, hyperlinks provide a resource for connection and disconnection (e.g. of elements, subject domains, authors and sites).

3.1.2 Multimodal ensembles

Image, action, sound and other modes (including the body) are entwined in new multimodal configurations, often in a struggle for meaning. The classical relationship between image and word is discussed as either 'anchorage' (Barthes, 1977), in which the writing works to tie down the meaning of the image by helping the reader choose what is to be noticed, and in which the image illustrates the writing; 'reinforcement' through repetition, in which image and word do 'the same' thing; or as 'elaboration', in which image and word extend the meaning of one another. However, these concepts do not capture the full struggle between word and image in the contemporary context. Image and word are perhaps now more independent, often separated from one another, with a new relationship of distant connection. In the words of Mitchell, 'word and image are more like ships passing in the night, two storm-tossed barks on the sea of the unconscious signalling to each other' (interviewed by McNamara, 1996:27). Uncoupling image from language in this way opens up the educational space for the visual and its role in creativity and learning.

The visual is increasingly important in materials where writing is not dominant. This is especially so in digital configurations (Leander, 2007). Hypertext and layout - colour, font, framing devices, bullets, boxes and margins - appear to be emerging as forms of meaning-making in their own right, and are increasingly central to the work of interpreting hypermodal texts (Lemke, 2002; Zammit, 2007; van

Leeuwen, 2005; Bezemer and Kress, 2008). These resources can be used to create new layers of information in a text: separating or linking domains of fact and fiction, or science and the everyday; or juxtaposing texts to create tension, critique, similarity or contrast.

Multimodal configurations interrupt, fragment and unsettle the genres and forms of texts including textbooks, students' texts, the resources used on whiteboards, and software applications. The genre of 'edutainment' (Buckingham, 2007), for example, is realised through new combinations of image, word and animation. The textbook form, for instance, is changing with information re-organised into bite-size chunks. This is a modularisation process that can be seen as a pervasive response to broad social conditions realised in the management of information and attention across the curriculum (Moss *et al*, 2007; Jewitt, Moss and Cardini, 2007).

In his analysis of production software commonly used in image, video, music and animation work with young people, Sefton-Green (2005) shows the importance of understanding the multimodal ensembles of visual and other non-symbolic resources that are made available to learners (see Figure 6). Software applications make available resources for shaping knowledge, and represent what it is that is to be learnt, in ways that are significant for learning (Adamson and Jewitt, 2003). The design of computer applications structures *how* young authors think about the medium, and influences the process of making as well as what is created (Sefton-Green, 2005). With a focus on young people's creative media production, Sefton-Green examines how conceptions and conventions of the visual are remade by the functions of filters – special effects, layers, timelines and loops – and other forms of sampling, in software applications (specifically Photoshop, video editing programs and Flash). He draws on the work of Manovich (2006) to explore 'how digital technologies compose and create' through manipulating, selecting or combining blocks or 'units' of data' (Sefton-Green, 2005:108). This highlights the role of software in the provision of a pre-existing visual (as well as audio and animation) database of ready-made elements to the producer (i.e. images, sound effects or musical samples). Sefton-Green suggests that creative work can be considered as 'a series of choices from pre-given options' (2005:108) in which production software operates as a 'scaffold' to support the creativity of the learner. How this scaffolding is realised is therefore central to what the learner will be enabled to do.

The multimodal resources of digital materials place image in new configurations with action, in ways which re-make the boundaries between them and impact on the construction of knowledge and identities (Leander, 2007; Jewitt, 2006; Pelletier, 2005; see also sections 4.5 and 5.1).

Figure 6. *A young person at WAC Performing Arts & Media College London, using digital music editing software.* © WAC Performing Arts & Media College London

3.1.3 Image and writing

Substantial theoretical descriptions of the dynamics of interaction between image and language have been offered, for example, in the early work of Kress and van Leeuwen (2006) and in Lemke's work on science textbooks (1998). A study of Biology textbooks (Libo, 2004) showed that visual images extend and complement the language in textbooks, both in terms of their content and the interpersonal relationship they set out to establish with the reader. In his analysis Libo concluded that in order to understand the meaning of the text, image and writing need to be fully integrated. Visual communication in its many forms has been on the ascendant for many years, but fears for the visual suffocation of print literacy have been exaggerated (Goodwyn, 2004). Burn and Dixon (2005) point out that this fear has its historical routes in the desire to protect school English from a perceived 'corruption' of visual popular culture. In refutation to this fear, it has been claimed that image has not replaced word, but rather that image and word are in a new relationship to realise new social relations and functions demanded by the contemporary communicational landscape (Kress, 2003).

Recent work by Bezemer and Kress (2008) examines contemporary curriculum materials and investigates the gains and losses of different multimodal ensembles for learning. The study draws on a collection of learning resources for secondary school in Science, Mathematics and English from the 1930s, the 1980s, and from the first decade of the 21st century (see Figure 7a and 7b). It sets out to provide an account of changes to the design of these learning resources and of the nature of knowledge they contain as well as their social-pedagogic significance. Through investigating the relationship between image, writing, action and layout, Bezemer and Kress show that image and layout are increasingly meshed in the construction of content. They illustrate how the amount of images in texts, as well as the quality and function of images or animation in a text, is in a state of change. Images do not primarily function to illustrate or duplicate what is written on the page or screen. Rather image and word attend to discrete aspects of meaning. Increasingly, concepts are introduced, established and analysed visually, while writing is increasingly brought into new kinds of relationships with, or even exchanged for, visual and multimodal forms of representation (Bachmair, 2006; Jewitt, 2002, 2006).

The future of writing will become clearer with time, argues Lanham: 'The expanded palette of textual display offered to text [writing] by digital expression again and again pulls us back into the history of western notation. The whole weight of these alternative display modes recaptures this history instead of, as the media prophets of doom argue, repudiating it' (Lanham, 2001:7). Whilst acknowledging the transformation of materials by the combination of writing with other modes, Merchant (2007) also warns against overlooking the role of written information on screen-based forms. Even in the most visual of digital forms (such as YouTube), he argues that access and

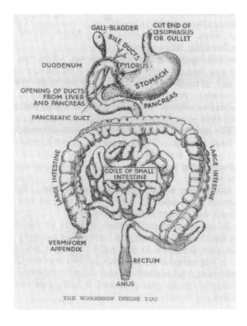

Figure 7a. *A page from, Allcott, A. (1952a). "Chapter III. Making Good the Wear and Tear of Our Bodies" pp 20-31 in Science for Girls. Book Two. London: Cassell. 20-31. A textbook analyzed as part of the project Gains and Losses: Changes in Representation, Knowledge and Pedagogy in Learning Resources directed by Jeff Bezemer and Gunther Kress (funded by the ESRC).*

Figure 7b. *A screen from the BBC website Bitesize (www.bbc.co.uk/bitesize) A website analyzed as part of the project Gains and Losses: Changes in Representation, Knowledge and Pedagogy in Learning Resources directed by Jeff Bezemer and Gunther Kress (funded by the ESRC).*

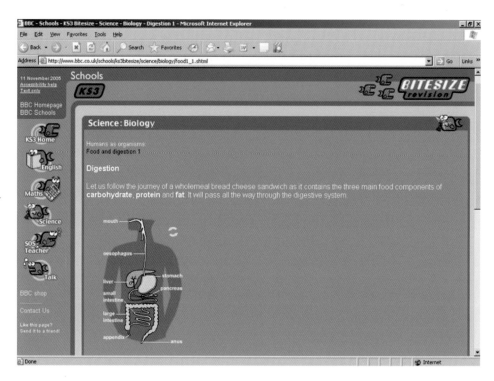

participation rely on writing and other symbolic forms in the form of commenting and rating (Merchant, 2007:121). Nonetheless, he shows that the forms and functions of writing on screen are changing: they are becoming less fixed and more fluid, more interwoven with other texts, with hybrid genres, new relationships to authorship, and fraying boundaries of knowledge. Carrington (2005) suggests that what may appear to be the maintained dominance of writing in multimedia games or the Internet masks a subtle change in its role. While an abundance of writing persists in games, its relevance to successful interaction is less direct. Playing a game requires experimenting, guessing and taking risks. In this context the written text offers an auxiliary source of information: visual information is brought to the foreground, a reversal of past relationships between word and image.

The new arrangements of image, word and other modes on the page and screen raise new questions for what it means to read, write, learn and be literate, and for creativity and learning more generally which are directly addressed later in this review.

3.2 Changing sites of display

In contemporary sites of education there is a gradual move away from a reliance on print as the *primary* medium of dissemination and instruction towards digital media and the screen (Boulter, 1991;

Kress, 2003). Interactive whiteboards, visualisers and scanners provide new digital spaces for display and collaboration. However, both print and digital media continue to play a key role in education. The 'new' connects with, slips and slides over the 'old': the screen is still connected with the page, present and past (Manovich, 2006), just as the page is increasingly shaped and re-made by the notion of the screen. There are screens that look page-like and pages that look screen-like (e.g. Dorling Kingsley books).

Discussion often focuses on the differences between the page and the screen as two distinct 'sites of display'. Often in these different sites, image and writing take on different functions and social meanings. The dynamic and ephemeral nature of print on the screen makes available particular functionalities, potentials for meaning and multimodal configurations that the permanent- linearity of print in a book seldom does. However, as Jones (in press) and Scollon and Scollon, (2003) argue sites of display are not only media they are 'social occasions' which make particular social interactions possible. This perspective raises the question of what people actually do with sites of display. It broadens the notion of 'sites of display' beyond books and computer screens, to include exhibition halls and shop windows among many others, and prompts us to question what people *do* with sites of display.

Sefton-Green argues that the screen has changed since the advent of the internet in the early 1980s. The screen, he states, 'is now more 'interactive', more dominant of the visual field', providing 'principal means of communication beyond the living room walls' (Sefton-Green, 2006:279). The changing character and multiple functions of the screen are considered by Walker (2006), with respect to screens in the museum landscape and the many ways in which screens can be designed. For instance, how screens are used to show visitors things too small to be seen with the naked eye; to create artificial environments and immerse people in an experience; to create surfaces to gather and interact around; to put lifeless artefacts into motion; to define space; to augment reality; and to personalise information. The mobile phone and other hand-held devices provide a new type of screen, a new 'point of delivery', that is changing how media and digital cultures insert into and constitute social contexts (Ito, Okabe and Matsuda, 2006). The new generations of mobile camera phones have implications for the role and function of the visual in the creation of personal narratives of everyday life and learning experiences.

The sites of display made available to children and young people, and how they are used, affects creativity and learning through the collaboration and interaction that these support and make possible. The decision to work on individual computers, collectively on an interactive whiteboard, or in an exercise book is a matter of the social design of space and interaction in the classroom. Two questions for educators interested in creativity and education are what kinds of social interaction are wanted in the learning space and how can screens be designed to support these ambitions?

3.3 New shapes of knowledge

How knowledge is represented, in which mode, and through which media, is crucial to knowledge construction. In other words, how we form representations is integral to meaning, creativity and learning more generally. The ways in which phenomena or concepts are represented shapes both *what* is to be learnt (e.g. the curriculum content), as well as *how* it is to be learnt (the practices involved). Image and other non-linguistic forms take on specific roles in the construction of school knowledge. For example, the representation of a cell in the science classroom as an image or through writing, in colour or black and white, or as 3D model or an animated sequence on a CD-Rom or webpage, makes available distinct aspects of the concept of the 'cell'. Image and writing, it has been shown, make different demands on the learner and have differential potential effects for learning, the shaping of learner identities, and how learners' navigate pathways through texts. The choice of form is central to content, and to how knowledge is shaped (Kress *et al*, 2001, 2005; O'Halloran, 2005). For example, previously discrete texts (e.g. novels, poems etc.) for study have now been made available online. In this process, printed text is repackaged with image, animation and sound, digitally annotated, fragmented, and connected via hyperlinks to author biographies and other historically and socially relevant knowledge, becoming part of a larger web of texts. This further remakes the authority of texts, unsettles the boundaries and forms of knowledge, and creates connections across previously distinct boundaries. The relationship between consumption and production is remade or blurred, and the fluid connectivity of the turn to the visual erodes boundaries across domains and disciplines.

The active engagement of the reader is highlighted by the turn to the visual. Words and image encourage readings that reject a single interpretation and instead hold in suspense the possibility of multiple readings co-existing alongside each other. Hyperlinks are key in this process of breaking down and fraying textual boundaries, by creating new connections beyond the text. In this way, hyperlinks are a 'technological fait accompli' for the death of the author (Harper, cited in Neilsen, 2001:203). Through this breakdown, diverse relations between authority and knowledge are realised. The advent of user-generated content is one outcome of the intersection of digital production and newly made forms of authorship. The ease of producing and disseminating visual narratives of events has enabled low-grade digital photographs and video footage from mobile phones and camcorders to move across the domains of domestic photography and into a variety of public broadcast domains, including mainstream news and television. Theorists argue that this has unsettled traditional shapes of knowledge and what these demand of viewers, as well as who is sanctioned to produce and disseminate knowledge.

New shapes of knowledge reposition the learner in relation to knowledge, in particular transforming their role in the authentication, evaluation and selection of information. This foregrounds the active ideological work of making meaning:- in these new distributions of power and agency, knowledge is produced rather than acquired. However, the value of the knowledge that users generate depends on the context of its use and there have been concerns that in many cases there is merely the reduplication of information rather than the creation of new knowledge.

The creation of user-generated content is a central aspect of technologised production practices for pedagogy. Different forms of production are required that allow students to generate and produce their own responses. Student production is an important aspect of student work in the classroom and research has repeatedly shown the value of production as a kind of externalisation in supporting learning. The work of production forces learners to express their thinking, thereby making the gaps in their knowledge explicit, and clarifying what they need to learn.

Some projects have made use of mobile and internet technologies to support children in authoring visual and multimodal narratives. Often these link a field experience, gallery or museum visit with the school[11]. Children use these technologies to collect and produce photographs, drawings, writing and audio commentaries as well as museum and gallery objects. These can be manipulated, organised and annotated to produce personalised 'galleries' of a museum or gallery exhibition, multimedia diaries, documentaries, narratives and so on. This works to create connections across time and space (as well as distinct experiences), and enables narratives to be circulated, shared, reused and further transformed (see Figure 8). New technologies offer learners the means to manipulate information in ways that significantly re-shape knowledge: that is what is to be learnt as well as how it is to be learnt (Price and Rogers, 2003; Walker, 2007).

---

[11] Example projects include, MyArtSpace, Mudlarking, Ambient wood, and Savannah. Please see references for details.

Figure 8. *A student captures interpretive information to use for group research, in the Palm House at Kew Gardens, London. Photograph by Kevin Walker taken as part of his research on mobile technologies and museums (Walker, 2007).*

3.4 New conditions and functions for authorship

Practices of production and dissemination have been transformed by new technologies in ways that remake the conditions and functions of authorship and audience (Adkins, 2005; Lury, 1993). Both new media and multimodality have an interest in understanding the practices of young people as creative producers. In the changing landscape of the visual turn there is a sense that digital technologies, and visual communication more generally, offer young people new forms of power and agency within the communicational landscape.

Sefton-Green (2005) notes, however, that in reality there is considerable debate on the extent of this new-found authorship. The debate is to some extent fuelled by different notions of consumption and production. What is apparent are the changing conditions and functions of authorship, in which remixing or mashing information blurs the distinction between consumption and production. Remixing involves 'selecting, cutting, pasting and combining resources into new digital and multimodal texts – achieved by downloading and uploading files from different sources (internet, iPod, DV-camera, sound recordings)' (Erstad *et al*, 2007). Jenkins (2006) describes these processes as a kind of culture of appropriation:

> *Appropriation may be understood as a process that involves both analysis and commentary. Sampling intelligently from the existing cultural reservoir requires a close analysis of existing structures and latent potential meanings. Often re-mixing involves the creative juxtaposition of materials that otherwise occupy very different cultural niches (Jenkins, 2006:33).*

This produces what Sefton-Green terms 'creative consumption', an intermediate kind of production involving the downloading, remixing and manipulation of existing content (2005:293). In their survey of American teenagers' use of social media, Lenhart and colleagues (Lenhart, *et al*, 2007) suggest that content creation by teenagers is continuing to grow, with 64 per cent of online teenagers (aged 12 to 17 years) engaging in at least one type of content creation. Girls continue to dominate most elements of content creation, with a third of online teen girls engaged with blogging compared with one fifth of online boys. This gender difference is similar with respect to the posting of online photographs, although boys post double the video content online than girls. The survey found that 'content creation is not just about sharing creative output; it is also about participating in conversations fuelled by that content' (Lenhart, *et al*, 2007:16). However, in a UK survey of children's online activity, Livingstone and colleagues (Livingstone *et al*, 2005) emphasised that complex skills are needed to effectively utilise the internet[12]. They suggest that the majority of children and young people in the UK are consumers of content, with only a small minority interacting with this content and even fewer creating it.

The question of who gets to be an author is remade in the contemporary landscape. However, children's skills and experiences of the Internet vary for boys and girls, and across different social classes. Middle class children are more 'likely to experience the Internet as a useful, if risky, medium than less privileged children (Livingston and Bober, 2004:415). Livingstone and colleagues emphasise the need for educators to avoid making universal generalisation about the access that learners have to different resources (such as the Internet), shaped as this is by an uneven landscape of class and gender. Nonetheless, new conditions of authorship raise important questions for education and where it draws the line between active consumption and production of knowledge.

---

[12] The national survey involved a total of 1,511 young people aged between 9 and 19 years old.

3.5 Visual production and dissemination

Digital tools have fundamentally changed media production and dissemination. As Erstad *et al* (2007) explain, 'the digitization of a wide range of media, computer capability and high band-width Internet connection imply that more students can work collaboratively with photos, sound, text and moving images using standard editing software' (2007). These tools provide new opportunities for learners making media (Sefton-Green, 2005; Burn and Parker, 2003; Burn and Durran, 2006; Pelletier, 2005). Broadcasting and production is made possible for children and young people in new ways through the internet, digital photography and video equipment and editing software (Sefton-Green, 2006; Lam, 2006; Bachmair, 2006). This has been called a 'kind of production renaissance' (Sefton-Green, 2005: 296), although currently children and young people have limited access to some forms of production and dissemination in many schools (Erstad *et al*, 2007; Knobel and Lankshear, 2006). Further, when technologies are co-opted by the school they are often used by teachers and students in reductive ways and adapted to fit with existing school practices and purposes (Owen *et al*, 2006; Lankshear and Knobel, 2003; Sinker, 2000).

Attention to visual and digital technologies serves to collapse, remake and blur the boundaries between consumption, production and dissemination in significant ways for creativity and learning. Information flows between producer and consumer are increasingly multidirectional and made complex by the use of digital technologies and the 'creation of grass roots cross-cultural and cross-boarder networks and creative techniques' (Lam, 2006:218) such as Anime and Manga. These boarder crossings create new challenges for mainstream production and copyright 'through the increasing transgression of the role of passive end users of media products' (Lam, 2006: 218). In a study of boys' (aged 5-7 years old) multimodal practices of making texts in the home, Pahl (2003) illuminates these collapsing boundaries in the meanings children construct. She demonstrates how young children consume and appropriate Pokemon and Yugio characters across television, film and game-cards, as well as how they visually make and remake the features of these global characters in their own cards and localised activities (see Figure 9). Against this backdrop, multimedia production can increasingly be seen as a process in which the negotiation and understanding of meaning is played out.

The notion of 'design' (see New London Group, 1996; and Kress, 2000) might prove useful here. Design refers to an active and dynamic process central to communication in contemporary society. Design refers to how people make use of the resources that are available to them at a given moment and a specific communicational environment in order to realise their interests. It foregrounds the importance of the interaction between multimodal resources, the sign maker's social purpose and intentions, context, and the potential audience (Kress, 2000, 2003). The New London Group (1996) draw on design to understand the multimodal organisation of social relations through the design of communicative resources, including linguistic meaning, visual meaning, audio meaning, gestural and spatial meaning.

A key aspect of changing modes of dissemination is the new form of social networks that are available to a broad range of people. Technology has transformed how information can be stored, shared and distributed between people and across learning situations (e.g. inexpensive portable devices such as USB vaults and memory cards), and sites that provide online spaces for sharing, storing and distributing information – such as Flickr, Bebo, YouTube, Facebook and Myspace, Blogs, Wiki's (Davies, 2006). Laptops, Internet, email, mobile and other hand-held devices, video conferencing, wireless networks, and virtual learning environments (VLEs) have the potential to distribute knowledge and to connect learners in new ways, to enable knowledge to circulate across time differently in online spaces, to archive and store data, as well as create complex rhythms of asynchronous and synchronous tasks and new economies of rhythm (Leander, 2007). MSN and online virtual communities offer new possibilities for collaboration, connection and participation.

Sefton-Green argues that this has 'unlocked a conundrum central to democratic aims of mass education across the developing world: that many can now communicate with many' (Sefton-Green, 2005:283). Through children's engagement with multimedia collaborative authoring and other activities, technologies of dissemination serve to exchange ideas and cultural products and to develop transnational ties (Lam, 2006:231). This potential is discussed in more detail in section 4.1 with reference to identity formation and management. New forms and patterns of participation are enabled by the facility of visual technologies to connect people, spaces, times and practices in new ways. These contribute to changing notions of friendship and an expanded space of connection for many (though not all) young people, thereby remaking experiences of knowing and being known. The potentials for collaboration are, however, constrained by economic, social and political structures that impact on the possibilities for democratic participation and other forms of social exclusion (for example, those who do not attend school for a variety of complex reasons). This raises issues of ethics, risk and safety, privacy and control over identity and participation. The new contexts and purposes for posting images, video and writing in these spaces also serve to remake the boundaries between private and public. This is compounded by the difficulty of removing images and other forms of information from the Internet, images that are circulated widely, recycled and collectively owned.

The changes in practices of consumption, production and dissemination raise a number of questions for creativity and education. In what ways can we ensure that young people's use of technologies goes beyond presentation and display? How can we design learning environments to disrupt simple transmission and create flows of information and ideas? How could the technologies that students routinely carry and use in schools in non-legitimated ways (e.g. mobile phones with cameras, MP3 players, game consoles) be used productively to support learning through the generation and dissemination of content? A particularly important issue for creativity and education is how to better theorise and describe the breadth of children's production practices and the multimodal mediascapes that they inhabit, and in doing so, to imagine how (and if) these can be taken up for the purposes of education and creativity.

3.6 New skills and practices

3.6.1 Manipulation and remixing

The manipulation of image, sound and video and so on, is often discussed in terms of 'mashing' or 'remixing' and has led to a variety of practices of production that are central to creativity and learning in the contemporary landscape. Manovich (2005) has argued that digital remixing is an activity that has precedents in modern electronic music from the 1980s, as well as the borrowing and reworking forms and styles from other cultures more generally. He writes, 'culture has always been about remixability - but now this remixability is available to all participants of Internet culture' (Manovich, 2005). Remixing is supported by digital editing and manipulation software together with the increased ease of locating and reusing material. Manovich locates this activity within deeper trends in modern industrial society, especially the rise of mass production and mass modularity in which parts are standardised to fit with other parts. He argues that with the advent of digital technologies, modularity is a principle in large-scale cultural production and distribution through the sampling and commodification of music, film and games.

Leander and Frank (2006) conducted research on the use of images in the everyday digital literacies of young people with a specific focus on social practices of identity in online and offline contexts. One objective of the research was to understand how young people relate to images emotionally and aesthetically (and how this is itself a social and cultural production), and researchers focused on how young people valued the ways in which visual elements can be combined and juxtaposed. One case study focuses on a student who 'remixes, modifies, and trades images to build a website for a punk rock band', while another case study focuses on a student who 'modifies and constructs images for online game-play' (Leander and Frank, 2006:185). The first case study student collected, selected, manipulated and assembled images to create visual texts for display on her computer, making new meanings from fragments – what Goodwin has called a kind of 'postmodernist sampling' (cited in Leander and Frank, 2006). This collection of images was transformed into a new project – a website for the band. This changed her private images into public ones, and the processes of remixing and redistribution opened up a space to form new affinity groups, share knowledge, and expand her discourse and design. The second case study focused on the design of character appearances (skins), by the student, in online games – involving the changing of body shape, eye colour and shape, nose shape, face shape, skin colour, shape and size of the body in an iterative process of design. The student later put these skills and expertise into practice in a collaborative development of an online game and the design and decoration of a virtual house. Leander and Frank argue that 'image aesthetics might function as a nexus for the social and personal in practices of identity' (2006:203). The ways in which young people design visual texts through their use of 'writing over, resizing, organising, and colouring images' is central to the visual connection of the local and global in shaping identities through social practices (2006:203). Both case studies highlight how the students engaged in processes of remixing to create a personal style from widely distributed resources and can thus be understood as productions. These productions are designed to be distributed and, in effect, build or mobilise new social communities (2006:204).

The creative potential in remixing is clear. However, it has been argued that it can lead to a culture of 'copy and paste literacy'. There is an additional tension with literacy practices within the school and the resulting view of these new media literacy practices as plagiarism (Perkel, cited in Erstad et al, 2007). Understanding the value of creative consumption and remixing in formal educational contexts as 'design' may help to resolve such tensions. As Maun and Myhill (2005) argue, 'these dichotomies can be positively and equitably resolved by conceptualising the text as an outcome of a design process, and thinking of writers as designers' (2005:6).

3.6.2 Interpretation and reading in a visual landscape

Recognising the multimodal character of texts, whether print-based or digital, impacts on conventional understandings of reading. Texts that rely primarily on writing can still 'fit' with the concept of reading as engagement with words. Reading is affected by the spatial organisation and framing of writing on the page, and the directionality, shape, size and angle of a script (Kenner, 2004). In this way, 'different scripts can be seen as different modes, giving rise to a variety of potentials for meaning-making' with different 'representational principles' underlying each writing system (Kenner and Kress, 2003:179). In other words, both writing and reading are multimodal activities.

The reading of visuals in children's literature has been the focus of much research. Kress (1997; 2003) and Kress and van Leeuwen (2006) outline why the reading of image is different from the reading of writing by describing the 'logics' that inform these two forms of representation. According to Kress, the logic of image and writing differ in significant ways for reading: the logic of image involves the presentation of space and simultaneity while the logic of writing involves time and sequence. The former foregrounds the arrangement and display of elements, and the work of reading is on identifying salience and connection. The latter relies on clause structures and sequencing.

Walsh (2003) undertook a study of the responses of kindergarten children (age 5 and 6) to two narrative picture books. The children's oral responses were recorded during both whole-class and individual reading sessions. These responses were analysed to determine which were specific to the written or visual aspects of the books. All of the children's responses were found to be responses to images, although some were a response to words as well. The children responded to the pictures and used them to understand and re-tell the story, including labelling, observation and comment. The pictures impacted significantly on the children's interpretations of the stories and 'the children were 'reading' – making meaning – with pictorial texts, regardless of whether they could 'decode' the words of the text' (Walsh, 2003:129). This study, along with many others (Jewitt, 2002; Bearne, 2003; Unsworth, 2001), suggests the need to reconsider the nature of reading in a communicational context where word and print are no longer dominant.

The multimodal character of the screen does not indicate a single entry point, a beginning and an end. Rather, it indicates that texts are layered and offers multiple entry points, presenting the reader with new potentials for reading a text (and the design of the text) through engagement with it. Reading a written text on a page is usually a linear event in which the author and illustrator guide the eye in a particular direction which is connected to the reading of a text. The reader is involved in the task of finding and creating reading paths through the multimodal, multidirectional texts on the screen - a fluidity that is beginning to seep out onto the page of printed books (Moss, 2001; Kress, 2003). Moss (2003) studied UK primary school students, working with junior age non-fiction texts as objects of design. She drew on a large data-set built up from a series of interlinked ethnographic research projects about reading between boys perusing non-fiction together in informal contexts within the school classroom. Her research shows how the layout structure of factual books impacts upon the way in which it is read by young boys. More specifically she shows how they sequence the page, create reading paths, negotiate their roles and identities in the classroom, and identify opportunities for performing 'being a reader'.

Digital technologies, as illustrated in the previous section on shapes of knowledge, have the potential to bring a wide range of multimodal resources into the classroom and to change the representations that students are working with. This impacts on learning as it changes the work of interpreting (and producing) resources in the classroom. Reading, whatever the technology, is always a matter of the reader selecting what she or he sees as being relevant. However, the multimodal resources, hyperlinks and different layers of content that are offered by new technologies serve to foreground this work (and sometimes make it more complex).

New skills and practices of information handling, management and analysis are demanded by the visual, and by the sheer volume of information that children and young people have access to via new technologies across educational spaces. Willams and Rowlands' (2007) literature review on the information-seeking behaviour of young people surveys a total of 86 academic papers in this field. Williams and Rowlands (2007) investigated a claim in the literature that the 'Google Generation' show a preference for visual information over text. The research acknowledged young people's 'strong liking' for the visual. The study concluded that on the one hand, 'text still rules the Internet' and on the other hand, that new forms of visual grammar and a proliferation of new visual forms and media are emerging (Williams and Rowlands, 2007:15). Drawing on a range of studies of reading practices in the UK, the review refutes the claim that information seeking and management are always eschewed in favour of visual media. Rather, they argue that where a specific learning task is set, young people's use of information technology almost ignores moving and still images in favour of text that can be printed and used to complete the set task. Importantly, however, when young people were under no obligation to find specific information, they often relied on images to infer the focus and usefulness of a webpage (Williams and Rowlands, 2007:15). This research underlines the need to engage with the diversity of children's media and technology experiences in the 21st century (Buckingham, 2007; Livingstone *et al*, 2005).

4 Visual futures

The previous sections have sketched the scope of the visual turn in education and the visual materials and practices that feature in this changing communicational landscape. These have also identified the themes that weave across this terrain and shape how people represent and communicate knowledge and experience in ways that are significant for creativity and learning. This part of this review moves on to ask what this reconfigured communicational landscape means for creativity and learning, with specific attention to: 1) new opportunities for learner identity formation and management; 2) literacy; and 3) teaching. The review concludes with a summary of the key points and challenges that a turn to the visual presents for creativity and education.

4.1 New opportunities for learners' identity formation

New practices of production and dissemination (see section 3.5) offer new possibilities for identities and processes of identity formation, and highlight the role of learner dispositions and identity management as part of creativity and education. Learning is increasingly discussed in terms of the creation of particular dispositions and orientations to the world. Further, success at learning is increasingly coupled with the ability to be autonomous and self-directed multimodal designers of learning experiences (Gee, 2004), to possess problem-solving skills with multiple strategies for tackling a task, and to have a flexible solutions-orientation to knowledge (Cope and Kalantzis, 2000). Lam notes that there is growing recognition that globalisation is creating 'greater fluidity and multiplicity in the identity formation of young people' (2006: 218). The importance of media and popular cultures as sites in which young people interact with diverse cultural materials and images, and develop social affiliations, is also widely acknowledged. Bachmair (2006) suggests that the cultural relation between people and contemporary media is undergoing a transition that is central to the construction of identities. In particular, he argues that media and its cultural objects are crucial in mediating young people's relationships to their inner world, their social environment, their world of objects and events, and the broader world of culture. Carrington stresses the need to 'acknowledge the ways in which we position children within these social practices and landscapes' (Carrington, 2005: 173).

Technologies open up new spaces for identity-play and for reflecting on audience and production processes, all of which are important for creativity and education. Technologies place emergent demands on the presence and performance of 'the self' in face-to-face, local and global virtual contexts (Butler, 1990; Bauman, 1998; Beck, 1992; Leander and Wells Rowe, 2006). Vasudevan (2006) explores how young people, in particular young black men, make and remake their identities in digital online and offline spaces, with a focus on their production of visual texts (e.g. photo essays and digital video stories). She analyses how the multimodal forms of expression made available to these young men in an informal out-of-school project, enabled them to author new self-identities and express multiple dimensions of their lives. Central to her work is an exploration of the way in which the visual can be used to create new spaces for storytelling.

Many online spaces are constantly in a state of being personalised, appropriated and remade. Online virtual communities (e.g. Bebo, Facebook, Myspace) offer new possibilities for visual collaboration, connection and participation, foregrounding the presence of new communicative repertoires centred on identity production and management. Interaction with online forums, YouTube, and social software sites, enable multiple 'identity categories' to be occupied and created (e.g. writer, reviewer, editor, mentor, summary writer, illustrator and critic). The production and maintenance of multiple identities is key to participation in a range of online learning environments that use avatars[13] (games, second life, some simulations). These require the design of image, movement, sound and speech to create a bodily presence on screen. Players design and use multiple avatars, switching between identities and playing with the notion of identity itself. The playing of online games - a popular activity for young people - embodies and enacts the negotiation of tasks and relationships in the creation of identities. The design of 'the self' involves the complex rendering of a range of modes into a multimodal sign. Identity formation and the construction of the literate-self are endlessly played out over sites and media, adopting specialist languages, leaving one world of experiences for another. This can be expressed as both a loss and a gain of new possibilities and new identities. Whether digital or physical, the design of learning needs to make clear both the potential gains of online learning, and how these are to be offset against what is to be lost (Gee, 2003; Kress, 2003).

Gee (2004) suggests that the societal conditions in many virtual spaces promote a collective sense of belonging, which he terms 'affinity groups'. Affinity group identities are developed by people networking, collaborating and affiliating around common interests, joint purposes and shared practices, to create new flows of cultural practice. Lam (2006) focuses on how the new flows of culture and learning in the context of globalisation impact on the literacy practices and identities of young people, for example, through their engagement with swapping and sharing graphics, images, manga drawings, videos and so on. Understanding how these transnational

---

[13] A digital representation that represents a person in chat rooms, IM programs, 3-D chat rooms and virtual worlds.

relationships and cultural practices enable a flow of diverse cultural material provides a way to understand the socialisation and identity formation of students.

These new opportunities for identity formation impact on creativity and education, and raise important questions for the kind of learners different sites of learning attempt to design, echoing the question posed by the New London Group (1996): what social future does education want to design for young people?

4.2 Rethinking literacy and learning

The turn to the visual, and the new configurations of resources, genres, practices and spaces associated with it, suggests a need to re-conceptualise writing and approaches to literacy within education. More broadly it indicates the changing requirements of communication and literacy in the 'knowledge economy' of the 21st century[14]. The implications for educational systems in knowledge-based societies differ significantly from those of the nation-bound industrial economies of the recent past. Yet the industrial/print nexus continues to dominate literacy policy and practice in schools (Gee, Hull and Lankshear, 1996; Gee, 2004). Against a changing communicational landscape, the dominant view of literacy as a universal, autonomous and monolithic entity is, at best, out-dated and in need of reconsideration.

A pluralised notion of literacy is needed in order to help students negotiate a broader range of text types and modes of persuasion (Morgan and Ramanathan, 2005). This makes it increasingly important for education to attend to the literacy practices of students and their diverse ways of making meaning, in particular the multilingual, visual and multimodal, and the digital. In short, there is a need to approach literacy practices as an inter-textual web of contexts and technology, rather than isolated sets of skills and competences. Because of the simultaneity of different modes in everyday community and educational contexts, the decontextualised study of linguistic practices, which assumes their universality and transfer, has clear limitations.

There is the potential to generate new forms of visual, multimodal and digital narratives, and other emergent forms of literacy that combine image with a variety of modes including blogging, culture jamming[15], and Web 2.0[16] practices (Marsh, 2005; Alverman *et al*, 2001; Leander, 2007; Unsworth *et al*, 2005; Cope and Kalantis, 2000; Lankshear and Knobel, 2003, 2006; Sinker, 2000). While the

---

[14] Powell and Snellman (2004:1) define the knowledge economy as 'production and services based on knowledge-intensive activities that contribute to an accelerated pace of technical and scientific advance, as well as rapid obsolescence. The key component of a knowledge economy is a greater reliance on intellectual capabilities than on physical inputs or natural resources'.

visual character of creativity, learning and literacy is clear, the question for educators is to what extent is education policy prepared to acknowledge this? And where do educators and policy-makers want to draw the boundaries between multimodal practices and writing (Burn and Dixon, 2005)?

Many kinds of literacies have been named as essential to communication in the 21st century, from digital to emotional. These literacies (and what to call them) are a constant source of debate within education. However, it is generally agreed that education needs to develop students' skills and ability to interpret image and to communicate visually (Unsworth, 2001; Buckingham 2003; Sefton-Green, 2006; Kress, 2003). Indeed Bolter (1998) argues that images, and the implications these raise for visual literacy, may yet prove to be the biggest question facing education.

The majority of the research projects and teaching interventions cited throughout this review are informed by the need to expand the focus of literacy to account for the aesthetic, creative and compositional aspects of the visual. Understanding students' mediascapes provides an important route to rethinking literacy and can open up a wider notion of learning (Sefton-Green, 2006).

Students in the classroom (as elsewhere) are engaged in making complex decisions about what mode to use and how best to design multimodal configurations. Even very young children are engaged in both the consumption and the production of photography and film in the home. For example, Marsh's (2003, 2005) ethnographic study of new technologies and the literacy practices of nursery school children (aged 2 and a half to 4 years), mapped children's mediascapes and patterns in media use through interviews, literacy diaries, questionnaires and home observation with 62 families. She also examined very young children's use of digital cameras to build narratives (Marsh, 2006). This work showed how the use of digital video, colour, props and spoken narratives made a significant contribution to the children's literacy development. She concludes that global media has a fundamental role in very young children's identity formation and the construction of themselves as literate. Further, global discourses of *Disney* and other popular brands mediate children's everyday literacy practices, demonstrating the increasing recognition of the complex interaction between the local and the global in these processes (Brant and Clinton, 2006). This study, and others, highlights the need to understand how children's literacy practices traverse physical, national and virtual spaces (Pahl,

---

15 Culture jamming refers to activities that attempt to undo and challenge cultural dominance and popular culture, often in a humorous manner, in ways that are unsanctioned or opposed by government or other powerful groups

16 Web 2.0 first coined by Tim O'Reilly in 2004 describes the trend in the use of Internet technology and web design to enhance information sharing and collaboration among users. Epitomised by web-based communities and services such as social networking sites, wikis, and blogs.

1999; Leander, 2007; Alverman *et al*, 2001). The empirical description of children's and adolescents' new mediascapes is essential to understanding how they negotiate social identity in relation to the economies and cultures of late modernity. Digital artefacts are key to the production of the family through the mediation of family activities and events, the recording of the family, as well as the construction of young people as literate (Buckingham and Sefton-Green, 2004; Rowsell and Pahl, 2006).

Similarly in his study of literacy and the visual, Callow (2005) suggests that consideration of images in educational contexts can 'open up and legitimate learning experiences hitherto glossed over or unexplored' (2005:15) and can offer students new routes into written literacy practices. Central to this is how the resources of writing are changed on screen through the foregrounding of choices of form, font and colour, the emphasis on design and layout, and the ease with which images can be utilised (Facer *et al*, 2003). Using these visual resources, children make explicit choices to convey meaning and to communicate their understanding of a topic in particular ways, not simply to make their work attractive.

The use of image and layout plays a central role in writing composition processes. Maun and Myhill (2005) observed 36 secondary school students, while they were undertaking writing in the classroom, and interviewed them immediately afterwards. The study explored the students' awareness of their processes of writing, and the linguistic and textual choices that they made. It found that these processes were multimodal, and integrated writing, image and other graphic elements. More specifically, Maun and Myhill found that students' perception of texts is formulated in response to its multimodal character: 'It seems that the visual appearance of the text acts as a gatekeeper to the text, conveying messages of accessibility or inaccessibility, and affecting readers' motivation to engage with the text: in other words, there is an integral link between the appearance of a text and the degree to which readers can engage in an intellectual way with it' (2005:13). Furthermore, they found the visual to be central to the relationship that these students set out to build with their intended readers. Students' perception of the importance of a visually attractive text was, at times, a tension within the process of writing, crossing words out, and moving chunks around, reducing the focus on the design through 'an unwillingness to make the text appear visually untidy' (2005:14). The study suggests the need to better understand, as well as to critique, how visuals contribute to the meaning of texts, in particular, the importing of generic clip art and borders. Attending to the meaning of what may be considered 'decoration' can provide educational insights into children's making of physical and digital texts.

A multimodal and social approach to literacy focuses on the representations of students across different sites of learning and raises questions about how curriculum knowledge is organised, classified, represented and communicated. It asks how different representations and modes of communication may shape, locate and connect knowledge in the world. It queries what teachers and students can 'do' with school knowledge, and how.

4.3 Rethinking teaching

The range of visual and multimodal resources, texts and technologies that come into learning spaces offer new possibilities and challenges for the design of teaching and learning. This, in turn, places new demands on teachers as the makers of texts and on how they orchestrate the resources, dialogues and activities across a session or lesson. New shapes and routes into knowledge are made possible, leading teachers to decide how best to respond to questions of authorship, authenticity and participation. The practices and dispositions that contemporary society requires of its future labour force also raise new questions for the design of the social relations of the classroom. These new expectations operate to transform the work of educators as well as learners, and remake the role of creativity within education. Furthermore, these new conditions remake the notion of education itself by blurring the boundaries and establishing connections between new spaces (and times).

Throughout this review, research projects have been described that build on young people's experiences and cultural forms of representation in order to engage with, and gain access to, student agency, cultural memory, and home and school learning, within local contexts (e.g. Marsh, 2003, 2005; Pahl, 2003; Sefton-Green, 2005; Stein, 2003; Walsh, 2003, 2007). Two further examples are briefly introduced here to suggest how the visual and multimodal can bring young people into a productive relationship with writing. Newfield and colleagues (2005) undertook a multimodal pedagogy intervention and research project, based in a Soweto secondary school, in order to develop the students' literacy practices. The starting point for this project was the literacy worlds of the students, infused with many different languages, cultures, music and performance not usually heard or seen in the classroom. These literary worlds provided the focus for poetry writing for the design and production of an anthology. The use of performance and visual arts opened up the voices of students who were identified as 'reluctant writers'. The second example, *A is for Arndale, A is for Atteridgeville* (Janks and Comber, 2006), is a cross-continent primary school project which sought to explore literacy through students' production of an alphabet

---

[17] This took place in two schools: one in South Africa and one in Australia.

book, drawing on their experiences and concerns of their neighbourhood (see Figures 9a, 9b and 9c).[17] The students were given the representations, examined, deconstructed and reconstructed, in a range of alphabet books with a focus on the design of image and word. The project developed students' design of a range of modes of representation in conscious ways, and the transnational context of the activity reshaped the pedagogic space and practices of social and cultural identities. Vincent (2006) argues that multimodal texts can scaffold students who achieve low levels of verbal expression in literacy, by providing them with a pathway that 'releases certain children from the trials of mono-modal, verbal expression where they are unlikely to succeed' (2006:56).

I is for Ice-cream Centre

The Ice-cream Centre is a place which one person owns. In the centre there are machine games like *Mortal Combat, Punisher* and games like snooker, pool and Jumpen. Every weekend celebrities come to perform and give us gifts and message about diseases like HIV/AIDS. The Ice-cream Centre sells ice-cream, sweets, chips and popcorn. We also buy ice-cream from the ice-cream van.

Figure 9a. *Page from Arndale – I is for IceCream (Janks and Comber, 2006).* © Hilary Janks

is for School Crossing

Outside our school gates is a schoolcrossing. We have school crossing monitors who watch the crossing beforeand after school.

My sister is in year 7 and she is a monitor. One of the monitors uses a whistle and the other monitors have broomsticks with hexagons with the word "stop" painted on it.

When the sticks are held up the cars and trucks stop and when the signs are down the cars and trucks go. This makes it safe for us to cross the road.

Figure 9b. *Page from Arndale – X is for school crossing (Janks and Comber, 2006).*
© Barbara Comber

While learning draws on a wide range of images and non-linguistic resources, mainstream methods of assessment used in schools persist in being almost entirely mono-modal (Jewitt, 2003). However, without an agreed schema for assessing multimodal texts, teachers are unlikely to accept them as a means of text production that can be judged and assessed. *More than words* (QCA/UKLA, 2004), is a guide to assessing multimodal texts, and offers a useful focus on the visual and textual element of texts, and provides an important first step in the process of assessment

X is for Xenophobia

In Atteridgeville we don't have problems with foreigners. Many foreigners have business in Mshengu Informal settlement. In some areas, like Soweto, Thembisa and Mamelodi they don't want foreigners because they accuse them of taking their jobs and being involved in crime. In some areas foreigners are involved in selling drugs. Some foreigners married South African wives and some of their children attend school at Banareng Primary school. We play with them and see them as children, not foreigners. We in Atteridgeville don't hate foreigners. We don't suffer from xenophobia.

Figure 9c. *Page from Arndale – X is for Xenophobia (Janks and Comber, 2006).*
© Hilary Janks

Conclusion

The focus of this review has been on image and other kinds of visual representations; the learning potentials of visual teaching materials and technologies; as well as the ways in which teachers and students activate and mobilise these through their visual practices and multimodal interaction in the classroom. Looking beyond language in this way raises many challenges and questions for creativity and education: What new visual and non-linguistic resources are available to learners and educational practitioners? What new relationships between the visual and the linguistic are made possible? How might these resources and relationships be exploited for the purposes of creativity and learning? What is the function of these in the contemporary social and communicational landscape? What does a young person need to know and do to be able to move successfully across this terrain? And what are the gains and/or loses for specific sites of education to move beyond language?

Against this backdrop, education (in its broadest sense) needs to attend to the specificity of how the visual is configured and elaborated (Virilio, 1994; Jay, 2002; Mitchell, 2002; Kress and van Leeuwen, 2006). The visual turn is central to contemporary notions of creativity and education. Those interested in creativity increasingly look beyond speech and writing to the visual and non-linguistic symbolic forms that feature in the multimodal mediascapes people (including children and young people) populate. In light of the increased attention to the visual it is perhaps important to recall that visual communication in its many varieties has always had a place in creativity and learning, including formal sites of education. This review set out to understand the present place of the visual across the contemporary context of creativity and education. The central focus has been on the visual but, as this review has illustrated, there is no pure visual mode and the visual is clearly just one mode nestled within the multimodal landscape. Therefore, in order to understand the visual, it is necessary to recognise and explore the ways in which image interacts with writing, speech, movement and other modes.

The foregrounding of the written word in education has been challenged throughout this review by a focus on materials and objects in the classroom and other learning contexts, and an attention to the broad range of images, film clips and so forth, that learners and teachers can quickly and easily access via new technologies. This establishes an urgent need for education to look beyond language, in relation to both the textual materials and practices of learning, and how the processes of learning are understood.

The broad range of resources that are available in the contemporary landscape are leading to the emergence of new multimodal configurations and genres (in both digital and print media) that are significant for creativity and learning (Kress, 2003; Jewitt, 2006;

Marsh, 2006). They are significant because of the ways that knowledge is re-distributed across image and other non-linguistic modes, as complex multimodal ensembles. Writing is one mode, image is increasingly dominant, and all modes play a key role in contributing to the meaning of the text (as discussed with relation to shapes of multimodal configurations – section 4.1 – and knowledge – section 4.3).

The need to link choice of form to content is a central theme running throughout this review: that is, how is knowledge shaped in epistemological terms? What can be done and thought with image, writing, or through action differs in ways that are significant for learning? In this regard, the longstanding focus on language as the principal, if not sole, medium of instruction can, at best, offer a very partial view of the work of communicating in the classroom. There is a need to move beyond viewing image and visual technologies solely in terms of information, processing and production, and to investigate how these resources shape learner identities, and relationships among learners (Luke, 2003; Lam, 2006).

The visual, even in the context of writing and composition, appears (not for the first time in history) to have taken a central position within the multimodal landscape of communication. The theoretical and pedagogic focus on a broad communicational landscape can support teachers in engaging with the resources that students bring into the classroom. This includes understanding students as sign makers, the texts they make as designs of meaning, as well as the meaning-making processes that they are engaged in.

A pluralised notion of literacy and teaching, which draws on a variety of forms of representation and communication, is needed in order to help students negotiate a broader range of text types and modes of persuasion (Morgan and Ramanathan, 2005). This makes it increasingly important for education to attend to the literacy practices of students and the diverse ways of making meaning, in particular the multilingual, visual and multimodal, and the digital. In short, there is a need to approach literacy practices as an inter-textual web of contexts and technology, rather than isolated sets of skills and competences. Because of the simultaneity of different modes in everyday community and educational contexts, the decontextualised study of linguistic practices (which assumes their universality and transfer) has clear limitations. As Bearne (2003) argues, what is needed is an educational framework that recognises and describes the new forms of text that children meet every day in order to secure the place of multimodal and visual texts within the curriculum.

References

Adkins, L. (2005). 'The new economy, Property and Personhood'. *Theory, Culture and Society*, 22(1), pp.111-130 (Special Issue on Inventive Life: Approaches to the New Vitalism).

Alverman, D.E., Hagood, M.C. and Williams, K.B. (2001). 'Images, language, and sound: Making meaning with popular culture texts'. *Reading Online*. [Available at **www.readingonline.org/newliteracies/lit_index.asp?HREF=action/alvermann/index.html;** Accessed 14.01.08].

Ambient Wood Project see **http://www.equator.ac.uk/index.php/articles/626).**

Appadurai, A. (1990). 'Disjuncture and Difference in the Global Cultural Economy', in Featherstone, M. (ed) *Global Culture - Nationalism, Globalization and Modernity.* Newbury Park, CA: Sage. pp.295-310.

Bachmair, B. (2006). 'Media socialisation and the culturally dominant mode of representation', *Medien Padagogik*, pp. 1-36.

Ball, B. (2003). 'Teaching and learning mathematics with an interactive whiteboard', *Micromath*, 19(1), pp. 4-7.

Barthes, R. (1977). *Image-Music-Text.* London: Fontana.

Baumann, Z. (1998). *Globalization: The Human Consequences.* Oxford: Polity Press.

Baxandall, M. (1973) *Painting and Experience in Fifteenth Century Italy*, Oxford: Oxford University Press

Bearne, E. (2003). 'Rethinking literacy: communication, representation and text', *Reading, Literacy and Language*, 37(3), pp. 98–103.

Bearne, E. and Wolstencroft, H. (2007). *Visual approaches to teaching writing: Multimodal Literacy 5-11*. London: Paul Chapman Publishing and UKLA.

Beck, U. (1992). *Risk Society: Towards a New Modernity*. London: Sage.

Berger, J. (1972). *Ways of Seeing*. London: BBC.

Bezemer, J. and Kress, G. (2008). 'Writing in Multimodal Texts: A social Semiotic Account of Designs for learning', *Written Communication*, 25(2), pp. 166-195.

Boulter, J.D. (1991). *Writing Space: The Computer, Hypertext, and the History of Writing.* Hillsdale, N.J.: Lawrence Erlbaum Associates.

Buckingham, D. (2003). *Media education: literacy, learning and contemporary culture.* Cambridge: Polity Press.

Buckingham, D. (2007). *Beyond technology: children's learning in the age of digital culture.* Cambridge: Polity Press.

Buckingham, D. and Sefton-Green, J. (2004). 'Gotta catch 'em all: Structure, agency or pedagogy in children's media culture', in Tobin, J. (ed.) *Nintentionality: Pikachu's Global Adventure: the rise and fall of Pokemon.* Durham, NC: Duke University Press.

Burke, C. (2007). 'The View of the Child: Releasing 'visual voices' in the design of learning environments', *Discourse*, 28(3), pp. 359-372.

Burn, A, and Dixon, H. (2005). 'English and the visual: from montage to manga', *English Teaching: Practice and Critique*, 4(1), pp.1-5.

Burn, A. and Durran, J. (2006). 'Digital Anatomies: Analysis as Production in Media Education', in Buckingham, D. and Willet, R. (eds.) *Digital Generations: Children, Young People, and the New Media*. London: Routledge, pp. 273-293.

Burn, A. and Parker, D. (2003). 'Tiger's Big Plan: Multimodality and the moving image', in Jewitt, C. and Kress, G. (eds.) *Multimodal Literacy*. New York: Peter Lang, pp. 56-72.

Butler, J. (1990). *Gender Trouble: Feminism and the Subversion of Identity*. London: Routledge.

Callow, J. (2005). 'Literacy and the visual: broadening our vision', *English Teaching: Practice and Critique*, 4(1), pp. 6-19.

Carrington, V. (2005). 'Txting: the end of civilization (again)', *Cambridge Journal of Education*, 35(2), pp 161-175.

Castells, M. (2001). *The Internet Galaxy: reflections on the Internet, business, and society*. Oxford: Oxford University Press.

Cope, B. and Kalantzis, M. (eds.) (2000). *Multiliteracies: literacy learning and the design of social futures*. London: Routledge.

Daniels, H. (2001). *Vygotsky and Pedagogy*. London: RoutledgeFalmer.

Davies, J. (2006). 'Affinities and Beyond! Developing Ways of Seeing in Online Spaces', *E-learning*, 3(2), pp.217-234.

Elkins, J. (2003). *Visual studies: a skeptical introduction*. New York: Routledge.

Erstad, O., Gilje, O. and de Lange, T. (2007). 'Re-mixing multimodal resources: ultiliteracies and digital production in Norwegian media education', *Learning, Media and Technology*, 32(2), pp. 183-198.

Facer, K., Furlong, J., Furlong, R. and Sutherland, R. (2003). *ScreenPlay: children and computing in the home*. London: RoutledgeFalmer.

Flewitt, R. (2006). 'Using video to investigate preschool classroom interaction: education research assumptions and methodological practices', *Visual Communication*, 5 (1), pp. 25-50.

Foucault, M. (1977). *Discipline and Punish: The Birth of the Prison*. New York: Vintage.

Franklin, S. (2006). 'VAKing out learning styles – why the notion of 'learning styles' is unhelpful to teachers', *Education 3-13*, 34(1), pp. 81-87.

Gardner, H. (1983). *Frames of mind: the theory of multiple intelligences*. New York: Basic Books.

Gardner, H. (1999). *Intelligence reframed: Multiple intelligences for the 21st century*. New York: Basic Books.

Gee, J.P. (2003). *What video games have to teach us about learning and literacy*. New York: Palgrave Macmillian.

Gee, J.P. (2004). *Situated Language and learning: a critique of traditional schooling*. London: Routledge.

Gee J.P. Hull, G. and Lankshear, C. (1996). *The New Work Order: behind the language of the new capitalism*. Sydney: Allen & Unwin.

Glover, D., Miller, D., Averis, D, and Door, V. (2005). 'The interactive whiteboard: a literature survey' *Technology, Pedagogy and Education*, (14)2, pp. 155-170.

Goffman, E. (1979). *Gender Advertisements*. London: Macmillan.

Goodwyn, A. (2004). *English Teaching and the Moving Image.* London: RoutledgeFalmer.

Grosvenor, I. (2007). 'From the 'Eye of History' to 'a Second Gaze': The Visual Archive and the Marginalized in the History of Education' *History of Education*, 36(4-5), pp. 607-622

Grosvenor, I., Lawn, M. and Rousmaniere, K. (eds.) (1999). *Silences and Images: The social history of the classroom.* New York: Peter Lang.

Hall, S. (ed.) (1997). *Representation: Cultural Representations and Signifying Practices.* London: Sage.

Ito, M., Okabe, D. and Matsuda, M. (eds.) (2006). *Personal, Portable, Pedestrian: Mobile phones in Japanese life.* Cambridge, MA: MIT Press.

Janks, H. and Comber, B. (2006). 'Critical literacy across continents', in Rowsell, J and Pahl, K. (eds.) *Travel Notes from the New Literacy Studies: Instances of Practice.* Clevedon: Multilingual Matters Ltd, pp. 95-119.

Jay, M. (2002). 'That visual turn: The advent of visual culture', *Visual Culture*, 1(1), pp. 87-92.

Jenkins, H. (2006). 'Learning By Remixing'. Guest blog available online at: **http://www.pbs.org.mediashift/2006/07/learning_by_remixing.html** [accessed 14.01.08].

Jenks, C. (1995). *Visual Culture.* London: Routledge.

Jewitt, C. (2002). 'The move from page to screen: the multimodal reshaping of school English', *Journal of Visual Communication*, 1(2), pp 171-196.

Jewitt, C. (2003). 'Multimodality and computer mediated learning', in Jewitt, C., and Kress, G. (eds.) *Multimodal Literacy.* New York: Peter Lang, pp: 34-55.

Jewitt, C. (2006). *Technology, literacy and learning: a multimodal approach.* London: Routledge.

Jewitt, C., and Adamson, R. (2003). 'The multimodal construction of rule in computer programming applications', *Education, Communication and Information*, 3(3), pp. 361-382.

Jewitt, C. and Jones, K. (2005). 'Managing Time and Space in the New English Classroom', in Lawn, M and Grosvenor, I. (eds.) *Material Cultures of Schooling: , design, technology, objects, routines.* Oxford: Symposium Books.

Jewitt, C., Moss, G. and Cardini, A. (2007). 'The interactive whiteboard phenomenon: reflections on teachers' and learners' responses to a novel classroom technology', *Learning, Media and Technology*, 32(3), pp. 303-317.

Jones, R. (in press). 'Technology and sites of display', in Jewitt, C. (ed.) *Routledge Handbook of Multimodal Analysis.* London: Routledge.

Kenner, C. (2004). *Becoming Biliterate: Young Children Learning Different Writing Systems.* Stoke-on-Trent: Trentham Books.

Kenner, C. and Kress, G. (2003). 'The multisemiotic resources of biliterate children', *Journal of Early Childhood Literacy*, 3 (2), pp. 179-202.

Kennewell, S. and Beauchamp, G. (2007). 'The features of interactive whiteboards and their influence on learning', *Learning, Media and Technology*, 32(3), pp. 227-241.

Kerski, J. (2003). 'The Implementation and Effectiveness of GIS Technology and Methods in Secondary Education', *Journal of Geography*, 102(3), pp. 128-137.

Klein, P. (2003). 'Rethinking the multiplicity of cognitive resources and curricular representations: alternatives to learning styles and multiple intelligences', *Journal of Curriculum Studies*, 35(1), pp. 45-81.

Knobel, M. and Lankshear, C. (2006). 'Weblog worlds and constructions of effective and powerful writing: Cross with care and only where the signs permit', in Rowsell, J. and Pahl, K. (eds.) *Travel Notes from the New Literacy Studies: Instances of Practice.* Clevedon: Multilingual Matters Ltd, pp. 72-92.

Kress, G. (1996). *Before Writing: Rethinking Paths to Literacy.* London: Routledge.

Kress, G. (2000). 'Multimodality', in Cope, B. and Kalantzis, M. (eds.) *Multiliteracies: Literacy Learning and the Design of Social Futures.* London: Routledge, pp. 182-202.

Kress, G. (2003). *Literacy in the New Media Age.* London: Routledge.

Kress, G. and van Leeuwen, T. (2001). *Multimodal Discourses: The Modes and Media of Contemporary Communication.* New York: Oxford University Press.

Kress, G. and van Leeuwen, T. (2006). *Reading Images: a Grammar of Visual Design.* London: Routledge.

Kress, G., Jewitt, C., Ogborn, J, and Tsatsarelis, C (2001). *Multimodal teaching and learning.* London: Continuum Press.

Kress, G. Jewitt, C. Jones, K, Bourne, J., Franks, A., and Hardcastle, J. (2005). *English in Urban Classrooms: A multimodal perspective on teaching and learning.* London: Routledge Falmer.

Lanham, R. (2001). 'What Next for Text?', *Education, Communication, and Information*, 1(1): pp. 59-74.

Lam, W. (2006). 'Culture and learning in the context of globalization: Research directions', *Review of Research in Education*, 30(1), pp. 213-237.

Lankshear, C. and Knobel, M. (2003). *New literacies: changing knowledge and classroom learning.* Buckingham: Open University Press.

Latour, B. and Woolgar, S. (1986). *Laboratory Life: The Construction of Scientific Facts.* New Jersey: Princetown University Press.

Leander, K.M. (2001). 'This is our freedom bus going right now: Producing and hybridizing space-time contexts in pedagogical discourse. *Journal of literacy research,* 33(4), pp. 637-679.

Leander, K. (2007). 'Youth Internet practices and pleasure: Media effects missed by the discourses of "reading" and "design"', (Keynote) ESRC Seminar Series: Final conference *Play, Creativity and Digital Cultures*, 9 June 2007, Institute of Education: London.

Leander, K. and Frank, A. (2006). 'The aesthetic production and distribution of image/subjects among online youth', *E-Learning*, 3(2), pp.185-206.

Leander, K. and Wells Rowe, D. (2006). 'Mapping literacy spaces in motion: A rhizomatic analysis of a classroom literacy performance', *Reading Research Quarterly*, 41(4), pp. 428-460.

Lemke, J.L. (1998). 'Multiplying Meaning: Visual and Verbal Semiotics in Scientific Text', in Martin, J.R. and Veel, R. (eds.) *Reading Science.* London: Routledge, pp. 87-113.

Lemke, J.L. (2002). 'Travels in Hypermodality', *Visual Communication*, 1(3), pp. 299-325.

Lenhart, A., Madden, M., Macgill, R., and Smith, R. (2007). *Teens and social media, Pew Internet and American Life Project.* Information available at: **http://www.pewinternet.org/pdfs/PIP_Teens_Social_Media_Final.pdf** [accessed 14.01.08]

Libo, G. (2004). 'Multimodality in a biology textbook', in O'Halloran, K.L. (ed.), *Multimodal Discourse Analysis: Systemic Functional Perspectives.* London: Continuum, pp. 196-219.

Livingstone, S. and Bober, M. (2004). 'Taking up online opportunities? Children's use of the internet for education, communication and participation', *E-Learning*, 1(3), pp. 395-419.

Livingstone, S., Bober,M. and Helsper, E. (2005). 'Internet literacy among children and young people: findings from the UK children go online project', **http://personal.lse.ac.uk/BOBER/UKCGOonlineLiteracy.pdf** [accessed 14.01.08].

Luke, C. (2003). 'Pedagogy, connectivity, multimodality, and interdisciplinarity', *Reading Research Quarterly*, 38(3), pp. 397-403.

Luke, A. and Carrington, V. (2002). 'Globalisation, literacy, curriculum practice', in Fisher, R., Lewis, M. and Brooks, G. (eds.) *Raising standards in literacy*. London: Routledge Falmer, pp. 231-250.

Lury, C. (1993). *Cultural rights: technology, legality and personality.* New York: Routledge.

Lynch, M. (2006). 'Discipline and the material form of images: an analysis of scientific visibility', in Pauwels, L. *Visual cultures of science: Rethinking Representational Practices in Knowledge Building And Science Communication.* London: Dartmouth College Press.

Manovich, L. (2005). 'Remixability and modularity'. Available online at: **http://www.manovich.net** [accessed 14.01.08].

Manovich, L. (2006). 'The poetics of augmented space', *Visual Communication*, 5(2), pp. 219-240.

Marsh, J. (2003). 'One-way traffic? Connections between literacy practices at home and in the nursery', *British Educational Research Journal*, 29(3), pp. 369-82.

Marsh, J. (ed.) (2005). *Popular Culture, New Media and Digital Literacy in Early Childhood.* London: Routledge Falmer.

Marsh, J. (2006). 'Global, local/public, private: Young children's engagement in digital literacy practices in the home', in Rowsell, J. and Pahl, K. (eds.) *Travel Notes from the New Literacy Studies: Instances of Practice.* Clevedon: Multilingual Matters Ltd, pp. 19-38.

Maun, I. and Myhill, D. (2005). 'Text as design, writers as designers', *English in Education*, 39(2), pp. 5-21.

Mavers, D.(2008). 'The visualizer as a pedagogic site' presented at *Pedagogies for interactive technologies: IWBs and visualizers seminar*, WLE Centre for Excellence, Institute of Education: London. 8th February 2008.

McNamara, A. (1996). 'Andrew McNamara, Words and Pictures in the Age of the Image: An Interview with W.J.T. Mitchell', *Eyeline*, 30 (AutumnWinter), pp. 16-21.

Merchant, G. (2007). 'Writing the future in the digital age', *Literacy*, 41(3), pp. 118-128.

Metz,C. (1990). *Film Language: a Semiotics of the Cinema.* Chicago: University of Chicago Press.

Millard, E. and Marsh, J. (2001). 'Words with Pictures: The Role of Visual Literacy in Writing and its Implication for Schooling, *Reading*, 35(2), pp. 54–61.

Miller, D.J. (2003). 'Developing interactive whiteboard activity', *MicroMath*, 19(3), pp. 33-35.

Mirzoeff, N. (1999). *An Introduction to Visual Culture.* London: Routledge.

Mitchell, W.J.T. (1995). *Picture Theory: Essays on Verbal and Visual Representation.* Chicago: University of Chicago Press.

Mitchell, W.T.J (2002). 'Showing seeing: a critique of visual culture', *Visual Culture*, 1(2), pp.165-181.

Mitchell, W.T.J (2005a). 'There are no visual media', *Visual Culture*, 4(2), pp. 257-266.

Mitchell, W.T.J (2005b). *What do pictures want?* Chicago: University of Chicago Press.

Morgan, B. and Ramanathan, V. (2005). 'Critical literacies and language education: global and local perspectives', *Annual review of applied linguistics*, 25, pp. 151-169.

Moss, G. (2003). 'Putting the text back into practice: Junior age fiction as objects of design', in Jewitt, C. and Kress, G. (eds.) *Multimodal Literacy*. New York: Peter Lang, pp.73-87.

Moss, G. Jewitt, C., Levacic, R., Armstrong, V. Cardini, A., and Castle, F. (2007). *The interactive whiteboards, pedagogy and pupil performance evaluation* (Research report 816). London: DfES.

Mudlarking Project. Information available at: **http://www.futurelab.org.uk/projects/mudl arking_in_deptford** [accessed 14.01.08].

Mulvey, L. (1989). *Visual and other pleasures*. Bloomington: Indiana University Press.

MyArt Space. Information available at: **http://www.myartspace.org.uk/web/about. php** [accessed 14.01.08].

National Research Council. (2006). *Learning to think spatially: GIS as a Support System in the K-12 Curriculum.* The National Academies Press: Washington D.C.

Neilson, J. (2001). *Designing web usability.* Indianapolis: New Riders Publishing.

New London Group. (1996). 'A Pedagogy of Multiliteracies: Designing Social Futures', *Harvard Educational Review*, 66 (1), pp. 60-92.

Newfield, D., Andrew, D., Stein, P, and Maungedzo, R. (2005). 'No number can describe how good it was: assessment issues in the multimodal classroom, *Assessment in Education: Principles, policy and practice*, 10(1), pp. 61-81.

Norris, S. (2004). *Analyzing Multimodal Interaction: A Methodological Framework.* London: Routledge.

O'Halloran, K. L. (2005). *Mathematical Discourse: Language, Symbolism and Visual Images.* London and New York: Continuum.

Owen, M., Grant, L., Sayers, S. and Facer, K. (2006). *Social software and learning.* Bristol: FutureLab.

Pahl, K. (1999). *Transformations: Children's Meaning Making in Nursery Education.* Stoke-on-Trent: Trentham Books.

Pahl, K. (2003). 'Childrens' text-making at home: transforming meaning across modes', in Jewitt, C. and Kress, G. (eds.) *Multimodal Literacy*. New York: Peter Lang Publishers, pp. 139-154.

Pelletier, C. (2005). 'The uses of literacy in studying computer games: comparing students' oral and visual representations of games', *English teaching: Critique and Practice*, 4(1), pp. 40-59.

Powell, W. and Snellman, K. (2004). 'The Knowledge Economy', *Annual Review of Sociology* Vol. 30: 199-220

Price, S. and Rogers, Y. (2003). 'Let's get physical: the learning benefits of interacting in digitally augmented physical spaces', in Underwood, J.D.M and Gardner, J. (eds.) *Computers and Education: Special issue: 21st Century Learning: 43, 137-156.*

Prosser, J. (2007). 'Visual methods and the visual culture of schools', *Visual Studies* 22(1), pp.13-30.

QCA/UKLA. (2004). *More than words.* QCA/UKLA

Reid, M. (2003). 'Writing film: making inferences when viewing and reading', *Literacy* 37 (3), pp. 111-115.

Reiss, M., Boulter, C., Dale Tunnicliffe, S. (2007). 'Seeing the natural world: a tension between pupil's diverse conceptions as revealed by their visual representations and monolithic science lessons', *Visual Communication*, 6(1), pp. 99-114.

Rostvall, A-L., and West, T. (2003). 'Analysis of interaction and learning in instrumental teaching. *Music Education Research*, 5(3), pp.213-226.

Rowsell, J. and Pahl, K. (eds.) (2006). *Travel Notes from the New Literacy Studies: Instances of Practice.* Clevedon: Multilingual Matters Ltd.

Savannah. Information available at: **http://www.futurelab.org.uk/projects/savannah** [accessed 14.01.08].

Scott, P. and Jewitt C. (2003). 'Talk, action, and visual communication in the teaching and learning science', *School Science Review*, 84(308), pp.117-124.

Seaborne, M. and Lowe, R. (1977). *The English School: Its Architecture And Organisation, Vol II. 1870 - 1970.* London: Routledge and Kegan Paul Ltd.

Sefton-Green, J. (2005). 'Timelines, Timeframes and special effects: software and creative media production', *Education, Communication and Information*, 5(1), pp.99-110.

Sefton-Green, J. (2006). 'Youth, Technology and Media Culture', *AERA, Review of Research in Education,* 30(1), pp. 279-306.

Sefton-Green, J. and Sinker, R. (ed.) (2000). *Evaluating Creativity: Making and Learning by Young People.* London: Routledge.

Sinker, R. (2000). 'Making Multimedia', in Sefton-Green, J. and Sinker, R. (eds.) *Evaluating Creativity: Making and Learning by Young People.* London: Routledge, pp. 187-215.

Sontag, S. (1979). *On Photography.* London: Penguin

Stein, P. (2007) *Multimodal pedagogies in diverse classrooms: representation, rights and resources,* London: Routledge.

Stein, P. (2003). 'The Olifantsvlei fresh stories project: Multimodality, creativity and fixing in the semiotic chain', in Jewitt, C. and Kress, G. (eds.) *Multimodal Literacy*. New York: Peter Lang, pp.123-138.

Sturken, M. and Cartwright, L. (2001). *Practices of looking: an introduction to visual culture.* Oxford: Oxford University Press.

Unsworth, L. (2001). *Teaching Multiliteracies across the Curriculum: Changing Contexts of Text and Image in Classroom Practice.* Buckingham: Open University Press.

Unsworth,L. and Wheeler, J. (2002). 'Re-valuing the role of images in reviewing picture books', *Literacy*, 36(2), pp. 68–74.

Unsworth, L. Thomas, A., Simpson, A.M. and Asha, J. (2005). *Childrens' literature and computer based teaching.* Maidenhead: Open University Press.

van Leeuwen, T. (1999). *Speech, Music, Sound.* London: Macmillan.

van Leeuwen, T. (2005). *Introducing Social Semiotics.* London: Routledge.

Vasudevan, L. (2006). 'Making known differently: engaging visual modalities as spaces to author new selves', *E-Learning*, 3(2), pp. 207-216.

Vincent, J. (2006). 'Children writing: Multimodality and assessment in the writing classroom' *Literacy*, 40(1), pp. 51-57.

Virilio, P. (1994). *The Vision Machine.* Indianapolis: Indiana University Press.

Walker, K. (2006). 'Screens in the museum landscape', *Visual Communication*, 5(2), pp. 189-197.

Walker, K. (2007). 'Visitors' voices: Personal narrative trails', paper presented at the UK Museums Association conference, *Digital Dialogues: Using everyday technologies to personalize the visitor experience.* V&A Museum: London, 15 June 2007.

Walsh, C. (2007). 'Creativity as capital in the literacy classroom: youth as multimodal designers', *Literacy*, 41(2), pp. 79-85.

Walsh, M. (2003). 'Reading' pictures: what do they reveal? Young children's reading of visual texts', *Literacy*, 37(3), pp. 123-130.

Wiegand, P. (2001). 'Geographical Information Systems in Education', *International Research in Geographical and Environmental Education*, 10(1), pp. 68-71.

Williams, P. and Rowlands, I. (2007). *The literature on young people and their information behaviour. Work package II.* A British Library/JISC Study .

Zammit, K. (2007). *The construction of student pathways during information-seeking sessions using hypermedia programs: a social semiotic perspective.* Unpublished PhD, Australia: University of Western Sydney.